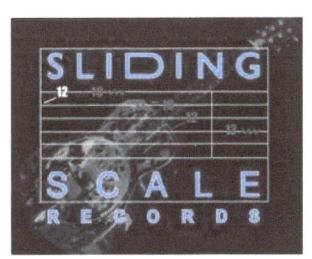

slidingscale.co.uk

Dedication.

To all those friends, known and unknown, who's hands and eyes are open to possibilities and to those who find themselves lost in many dimensions and those who struggle at times because of their dedication.

Publishing Data

First published 2014 Sliding Scale Books SSPB01a

Plaza De Andalucia 1, Campofrio, 21668, Huelva, Spain.

(c) Copyright Angie Scarr 2014
Text and step-by-step photography Angie Scarr 2014
Additional photography Frank Fisher
Design by Frank Fisher and Angie Scarr

ISBN 979-8-84453-299-3

All rights reserved

The right of Angie Scarr to be identified as the Author of this work has been asserted in accordance with the Copyright Designs and Patents Act 1988, sections 77 & 78.

No part of this publication may be reproduced, stored in a retrieval system or transmitted in any form or by any means without the prior permission of the publisher and author or her agents

The publishers and author can accept no legal responsibility for any consequences from the application of information instructions or advice given in this publication, or for errors, omissions or changes in formulae of mentioned materials.

Contents

Preface 5

Chapter 1: Introduction To Colour — 6
    How To Use This Book 8
    Limitations 9
    Choosing Clay And Colour Mixing Problems 10
    My Most Frequently Used Polymer Clay Techniques 12
    How To Pin Down Colours 16
    Colours Pinned Down 18
    One Man's Magenta 20

Chapter 2: Seeing Red — 22
    Powder Colours 24
    Red Is Not Just Red 26
    Cherries Project 27
    Tomatoes Are Not The Colour I Always Thought They Were ... 29
    Simple Rules For Making Miniatures 31
    Colour Bleed 32
    Colour Checking 33
    Lobster Colours 34
    'Pinky-Prawny-Salmony' Colours 35

Chapter 3: Mellow Yellow — 36
    Pigment Problems 38
    Mixing It Up 39
    Ageing And Ochres, Marrow Leaf And Assembly 40
    Designing Your Cane (Cucurbit Flower) 42
    Fine Flower Petals Using The Cut And Cross Method 43
    Yellow And Butter Recipes 44

Chapter 4: Colour Pages — 46
    Basic Colour Mixes For Common Clays 48
    Foundation Colour Mixes 50
    Brand Colours Mixed In Other Clays 51
    Angie's Colour Palette 52

Chapter 5: Green 54

Metamerism 56
Colour And Light 58
The Fimo Experiment - Results 58
Translucent Clays (Grapes) 60
Green Peppers Project 62
Bean Plant Project 64
Raw, Cooked & Overcooked 67

Chapter 6: Blue & Unusual Colours 68

Blue Is Rare In Nature 70
Peacock Feather Cane 70
Møns Klint Painting 72
The "Ugly Bug's Ball" 73
Colour Rules & Breaking Them 74
Mackerel Project 75

Chapter 7: Browns 78

Boletus Mushrooms & Setas 80
Autumn Leaves 82
Saving Leftover Clay 83
Brown Paper Bag Project 84
Wood Project 86

Chapter 8: Neutrals 88

Grey 90
Stone, Marble & Granite 91
A Trip To The Seaside 92
Finishes & Varnishing 93
Bacalao (Salt Cod) 94
Fish Skins 95

Chapter 9: Last Word In Colour 96

Opinions 98
Index 101
Biography, Thanks & Acknowledgements 102
Sources, Resources & Suppliers 103
Fashion & Polymer Clay 104

Preface

Preface to large format edition

Since writing The Colour Book things have changed massively in the publishing world. The original book was small format so that we, and our customers, could afford the postage. We were new to self-publishing and had a lot to learn. I do believe we crammed too much onto each page in an attempt to give great value by dealing with the whole large subject in one small book. We did make the size a benefit as people could pop that one in their bags so the idea of the colour bands on the pages, for identification and logging of colours came about. We did of course decide to keep the bands in the larger edition. This preface was written for the original handbag edition of this book. I have simply removed references to the little book.

I never went to art school. I never learned colour theory. I'm certainly no expert in colour.

I'm confused between print colours, light colours and the colours in my paintbox and polymer clay tubs, and that's just for starters! Why do I think I can write a colour book, even a handbook, for polymer clay users which helps them identify and mix the colours they see in nature? Sometimes doubts like this creep in. But then I remember that the best maths teachers are those that understand that everyone learns a different way and that many of us learn visually. There aren't many of those great maths teachers around because those who are good at maths themselves, don't seem to understand what it's like not to understand maths!

Well this is my attempt to draw the artistic out of what could be a very mathematical and dry subject by exploring colour in several different ways in the hope that you can pick out the bits that work for you. The art of seeing and recreating colour is a glorious and exciting journey. Some days we're more open to the subtleties of colour and the thing which makes us each and every one a slightly different artist is that we all perceive colour (and form) a slightly different way. In writing this book I have come face to face with my own colour 'demons' as you will see in the following pages. I hope this book will help you avoid the pitfalls. I hope it helps you look at and see colour from a few different angles and that it helps you appreciate that it's a much more complex subject than it first appears. And when a little stuck, will enable you to 'cheat' a little bit by giving you recipes to shortcut the analysing and experimentation process, but that in the end it makes you want to experiment and eventually cut out the slavishly copying process!

Fortunately, to help me along the way, I've had the artist's best equivalent of a tame mathematician: a 'computer geek'. My lovely supportive husband Frank has worked with me on producing the colour bands around which the book hinges.

Even though it's written with miniaturists in mind I hope there will also be a few nuggets for the wider world of polymer clay users and 2D artists.

In a way, this book is an exploration of my own mistakes along the way in the time I've been playing, then working, with Polymer clay which I can now say is more than half my life, and of the information I've gleaned in the process of putting this little book together. Writing it has certainly boosted my inspiration. I hope it will also boost yours.

Writing a book with current colours and 'definitive' recipes associated with them, was always going to be risky. But I'm used to that as each time I've written a book there have been major changes during and after the writing of the books. Please be aware that any colour mixes are subject to small and large changes as clay manufacturers tweak their offerings.

Angie Scarr, 2014 & 2022

CHAPTER ONE
Introduction To Colour

Recipe Key: 1 p21 (Pink Premo)   2 p19 (Garlic Pink)   3 p21 (Dark Purple)

4 p51 (Premo Ecru)   5 Dark Flesh   6 p52 (Dry Sage Green)

7 p53 (Interesting Leaf)   8 p51 (Premo Olive)   9 p21 (Pinky Purple)

How to use this book

Why find a colour match?
Getting nature's colours right requires a degree of self discipline that simply choosing a colour you like (for a jewellery piece for example) does not.

The colour bands across the bottom of each page are colours and their shades that I have identified from nature and colours which already exist as clays. I've tried to put them in a reasonably easy to find order but some may be slightly out of the sequence you might expect. Wherever they work in a project or relate closely to another colour I've put them by that colour where possible but still attempting to get a pleasing flow. Some pages contain extra colour boxes to amplify ideas with related colours.

I have tried to put projects, ideas, recipes and suggestions in the colour band where they are most appropriate but, of course this is not always possible. Several ideas are linked to others across different colour bands so I have either given page references or chosen to pull a piece into another colour band.

How the colour bars in this book were produced.
Some items which I found matches for were bought from supermarkets (e.g. mackerel, cheese etc.) some borrowed out of peoples fridges and many, as I am lucky enough to have a productive garden, were checked from life, fresh picked or even still growing in the ground. All were matched against the same CMYK colour chart and, although there will be some discrepancies, I hope they are at an acceptable level and can short cut your research when maybe you don't have direct access to, for example, a marrow plant in full flower!

Professional Tip
Always test bake your clay before making a big cane or a big production run. Clays can change even within a brand and mistakes cost a lot more time and money than test baking. And keep notes, sticking your test sample to them so you can look back in the future. Keep an A4 shoebox full of your notes and test bakes.

Professional Tip
Invest in sensitive scales! I use a little scale called a 'Palm Scale' which is perfect for test mixing and for small mixes where accuracy is needed. If you can get one accurate to 100ths of a gram like this one it means You can get really accurate small test mixes. Some really accurate colours with some of the denser pigments like blue can require 1 tenth of a gram. Without the 100ths you would only get an accuracy of plus or minus one tenth, which could be double, or half the quantity you need!

When experimenting with mixes if you don't have scales you can roll out your clay colours to an even thickness either using a pasta machine or two identical strips of wood, two knitting needles of the same size placed on either side of your clay and use a cutter to cut the required number of pieces . Almost any cutter will do, but your shape should allow you to subdivide into smaller pieces. All that matters is that you use the same thickness of clay when matching proportions of more than one colour.

Limitations of this book

What this book can never do is pin down the manufacturer's colours in time and say that they will never change. This just isn't possible as, because the user's needs are changing and as the art and craft of polymer clay changes, manufacturers respond in their many different ways. Sometimes changing a formula, sometimes adding or subtracting pigments in response to needs or discoveries. More about this in colour mixing problems on page 10.

This is not mainly a book of projects, though there are some to whet your appetite. So this book is best used in conjunction with other books on the subject or just as a reference to help when you are inspired to invent your own designs. We have another book in the series: Simple Mold Making.

What it does do is show you how to think about colour, some ways of matching colours and how to convert colour mixes (for nature at least) from one brand to another.

There are certain other limitations in producing a recipe book for colour that must be pointed out.

Without the use of sensitive scales any mix may vary slightly from the 'recipe'.

The 'Carres colours' suggestions, are the nearest matches I can find.

All artists see colour in their own way. This book merely represents my interpretation of the colours of nature as I see them.

Except where stated, all colours were matched by myself in the months of July and August 2013, and March to April 2014 in bright Spanish daylight and checked in diffused daylight in an internal light-well.

These are MY colour interpretations. I may have made errors either of judgement or actual errors in my interpretations or the logging of the colours of nature, original clay colours and colour mixes. I may see colour differently to you, or to the clay manufacturers and I do not claim any absolutes in my artistic judgement.

This is just a colour recipe book. Like all 'recipe' books you should tweak or alter the recipes to your own 'taste' and judgement.

Where the clay manufacturers have been able to help me, their colour judgement will appear in the basic 'swatch' colour mixes in the centre pages. Where they have been unable to help my recipes appear.

Choosing your clay

It's unlikely if you've bought this book that you've never seen or bought polymer clay before. So you may already have a favourite brand. And if asked, I think the answer to this is fairly simple: get the clay you can find most easily near you. It can be very frustrating if you've come up with an idea and just can't get hold of your favourite clay quickly and easily. So try the easiest one to get hold of first. If there's something you just can't get used to then try a clay with different qualities that suit you better. The clay you use should have a good translucent and should hold it's shape when caning or sculpting. But there's no reason you shouldn't have a mixture of clays on the go. My workshop has all the major clay brands and some minor ones. I don't often reject a clay completely. Just find a property which that clay has that no others have. And interestingly they are all very

different! When you have explored one, have a go with another. Some clays have a slightly 'Non-Newtonian' property similar to cornflour, some have a waxy feel, one I've tried had a rubbery feel. For a complex cane I wouldn't put them side by side with a clay that flows more smoothly when it's being stretched. But I sometimes mix them to get modified properties. Although for legal reasons I can't advise mixing brands, there should be no danger in mixing clays as the onus is on the clay companies to make sure that in all normal and foreseeable use their product is safe. It is foreseeable that artists will mix clays. However if you are at all worried contact the clay companies involved and ask! Most of them now have a presence on social media. Most of them are happy to answer questions. If they aren't, and you're still concerned, you can avoid using their clay. Using clays with two different properties can add to the contrast. Just one or two words of warning. When making a complicated cane make sure you use clays that are the same softness and move in the same way. Some bake to a very opaque finish, some with a slight sheen and some oily. This can affect whether you need to varnish. And if so, your choice of varnishes.
See p93.

A word about baking temperatures.
When mixing clays it's probably sensible to try the lower of the recommended temperatures. Professionals, with separate well ventilated ovens, can experiment within the range suggested on the packs.

Colour mixing problems – pigments
One of the most important and exciting aspects of polymer clay is that it is available in many different colours and qualities. One of the most frustrating aspects is that the best

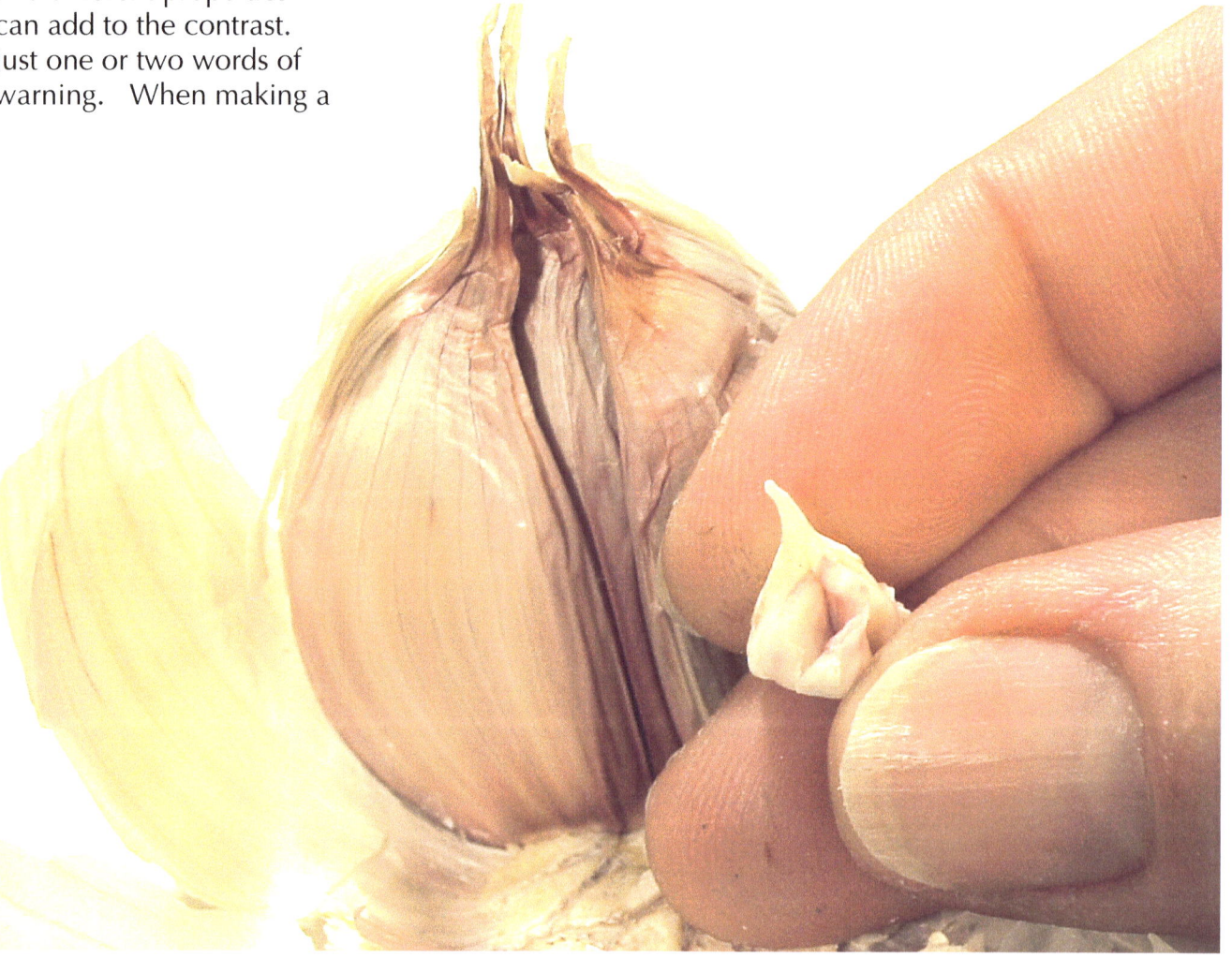

quality clays don't always come with the best choice of pigments, possibly because of financial constraints as some pigments are much more expensive than others, and also because of safety. Some pigments are just too toxic to use. All have slightly or greatly different quality of pigments translucencies and saturations. That is to say, the colours they put in can be of different quantities as well as qualities. Some manufacturers optimise their colours for the artist to choose mixes. Some want the brightest 'jewel' colours possible. Some are chosen for low toxicity if another choice would be more toxic, and it may be that some pigments have been chosen for simple economic reasons. It's worth pointing out that some pigments are radically more expensive than others, so this would be hardly surprising. Also not surprisingly clay manufacturers are loath to give information on their own recipes, so comparison of pigments, opacity/translucency and colour saturation has to be by experience. Another problem can be the relative opacity of some colours depending on whether the pigment chosen is an opaque or a translucent pigment and some can even vary from batch to batch because of pigment availability or slight difference of dosage. From time to time the clay manufacturers have to change their formulations and this can lead to slight alterations in the colour, luminance of the pigments and how opaque the extender pigments and fillers within the clay are. The colour has to be balanced with the 'feel' of the clay. This makes colour mixing interesting, exciting even but sometimes very frustrating.

Why have I chosen to ignore the manufacturer's standard bright orange and green colours?

Because polymer clay colours were first chosen for children's play use and then developed for jewellery makers, the manufacturers include bright jewel-like pigments which don't often have equivalents in nature. I have found most of the greens and oranges in nature are more successfully replicated by mixing down from the parent colours. It's as simple as that. That is not to say that there would never be a use for them. Just that they are on the outer edges of the colours I would choose to make up my palette.

It can be annoying to find for example, when trying to mix colours for nature, that many of the clay companies choose a rather 'fluorescent' looking pigment for their orange. When colour mixing from nature 'fluorescing' colours are rarely required. For example, I have never seen a clay 'orange' straight from the pack that looks anything like the skin of any orange fruit that I've ever seen.

This means some of the outrageously bright pigments usually have to be tempered a little or rejected altogether.

That said, some very interesting work is being done by polymer clay artist Lindley Haunani, using fluorescent colours to add a little 'punch' to normal colours when they seem a little dead.

Some amazing facts about colour.

The RGB (red green blue) model of colour production for printing produces 2 to the power 24 colours. That's 16 million variations.

CMYK Cyan Magenta Yellow Black produces 2 to the power 32 that's an incredible 4.25 billions of different colours of various hues tones etc. The reality is that most of us can only see between 1 and 10 million colours. But that seems to me to be plenty to be going on with!

Scientists have found a woman known as a tetrochromat, who sees 99 million more colours than others due to an abnormality in the number of optical cones. But don't worry. I've whittled all that down to a much less intimidating thousand or so usable colours for this book. There are areas I'd like to have left a lot more variations in, and there are limitations to my method which leaves gaps in tones you'll need to make up for yourself.

My most frequently used polymer clay colour techniques

These are the techniques I use because nature throws up these patterns over and over again.

Putting skins on things

This is a simple process and just involves making a really thin even skin (using a pasta machine ensures evenness) around a short fat cylinder of a lighter colour and lengthening it by squeezing and pulling and finally rolling to thin the skin out even more, then closing the ends over on both sides of a small piece to form a small fruit. The thinness and optical lightness of the skin adds realism to what would otherwise simply be a solid blob of clay.

Apple skin colour is Basic Spring Green on p48, add a little more white.

Lines and stripes: chestnuts, onions etc.

Simple lines (stacking). The skin process can be further enhanced by putting stripes into the skin, I use this on onions, rhubarb, garlic and chestnuts (shown). Put simply you make a 2 or 3 (or more) colour sandwich of the colours you need in proportions that will lead you to a pleasing and realistic result *(see cheating and exaggeration p31)*, cut that sandwich and stack up until you get, say, one quarter of the number of lines you need. Then slice and press together the slices to form a skin.

The skin is then put on the centre part, just as in the apples above. In this case, by leaving the end open, I'm using the centre colour as the end colour on the chestnuts.

Chestnut colour is on p82.

Insertion simple veins: radicchio

I use this technique for citrus fruit and for leaves particularly vegetable leaves. Put very simply I cut into a cylinder and insert lines, or in this case wedges, where I want them to appear in the finished smaller cane. When I have put the main veins in, I cut into the cane to add secondary thinner veins, note this cane also has a Skinner-shade to darken the edges.

See radicchio colour mix page 21.

Spots.
Wrapped spot, and inserted spot

There are 2 methods of producing spots in a cane. When making a spotted cane it isn't simply enough to wrap

one colour with another, cut and build up, as I used to do *(see 'trout' in my Making Miniature Foods book)* because this produces an irregularly shaped spot as the clay takes up the empty spaces between the cylinder. You need to shape the outside colour to fit together with the neighbouring pieces either in a random or regular pattern. If you want a large number of spots.

Or, if you only need a few spots, insert the spot as a thin cylinder into previously formed holes, one at a time. I use a knitting needle to form the holes.
See fig colour p21, dragon fruit colour p20.

Shading: the 'Skinner Shade technique', simple yellow asparagus
Nature produces some beautiful colour 'flows' through from one colour to another,

This is a really subtle one, but it's worth making a shaded block to cut the asparagus stalks from otherwise you could use powder colours to achieve a similar effect but this would be time consuming and less predictable.

The Skinner Shade technique (invented by Judith Skinner) is widely used throughout the polymer clay world to provide these colour flows between one colour and the next. These techniques are covered extensively in my book Miniature Food Masterclass.

See also p75 the mackerel project.

Pale yellow colour see p45.

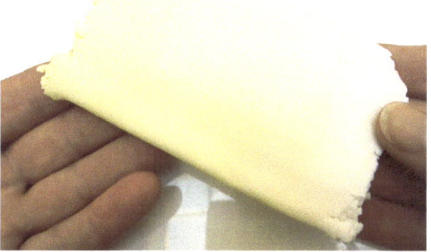

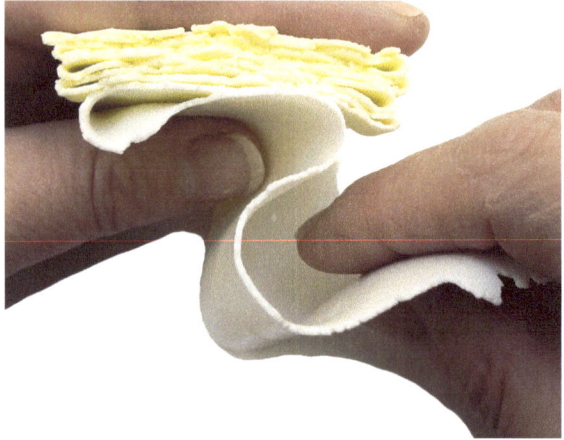

Shading, and stacking together

Blended stacking. To combine subtle colour flow with sharp edges to a colour change I often use the shading technique in combination with stacking. It's a way of 'smearing' into a sharp line. In music I would say it was like playing slide guitar. Dragging the main strong note from a subtly played lower note!

See pages 34-35 for more prawn and seafood inspiration.

'Offset stacking': leeks

This is an idea I stumbled upon quite by accident many years ago when I made a mistake while trying to fold a Skinner shade sheet together to make a block in the opposite direction as I was wont to do in those days before I discovered the wider polymer clay community! (most people make a Skinner shaded block by the method shown above) I put the pieces together badly and found the shades became shaded lines! It was another eureka moment for me. Of course I went back to stage one and exaggerated it. Nature does this even better of course. The same block is also good for spring onions. There are many forms like this in flower petals etc.

See leeks colour mix p58-59.

'Bleeding lines', simple or complex lines plus Skinner shade to mute the edges.

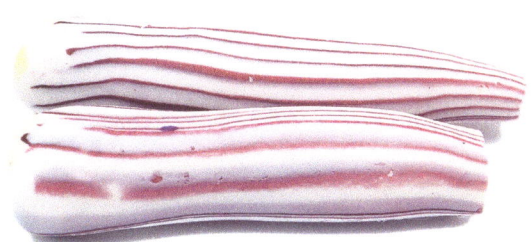

This is exactly the same process as making a striped skin (see chestnuts above) except that when you cut the slices for a skin and put them together you push at the lines in one direction to cause them to become slightly diagonal thus slightly covering part of the line with the other colour. This works especially well with semi translucent skins as in this garlic cane. It makes the lines slightly more subtle in a similar way to the blended stacking but without all the hard work. And there is a sense of the colour being there, but covered. I think this is a lovely, if a bit subtle, effect.

Lines through shades (strawberry)

This is just adding the 'inserting lines' idea to the Skinner shade technique.

Nature created a true beauty in the strawberry.
See strawberry colour p21.

Lines and spots through several layer shades (mackerel)

This project is shown in full on p75 and shows how you can achieve really subtle colour changes plus lines and spots all in the same piece. It's all a matter of taking things step by step and not rushing or taking short cuts.

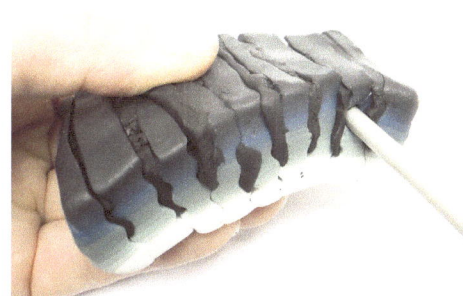

How to 'pin down' colours to use in later work

Often we're inspired by colours and forms of nature when we just don't have time to do the work, And then when we have time, the item is out of season. Taking photographs is useful but doesn't give enough information and is limited by colour reproduction which can be hit and miss,

Keep a notebook ... do a drawing ... take a picture.

When something inspires you write it down, like a diary. Say where you found it, when, what you would like to make with/from it. Pinning down the date helps stop you making seasonal errors. But remember supermarkets often stock items that were unavailable or out of season in the past, so be aware if you're recreating a scene from the past you may have to do some research on availability and in the case of fruit and vegetables even on cultivars. In the case of meat, whether the fashion at the time of your scene was to have cuts of meat fatty or lean. Even the way meat is cut varies not only from country to country but from epoch to epoch!

Take photographs or even pressings in the case of flowers. Write down dimensions but most importantly pin down the colours by matching as closely as possible with the colour charts on the bottom of this book, or with a method of your choice *see p18 & 19*.

Write down the reference for the colour next to the part of the picture. In the case of something having graded colours write the 'from' and 'to' numbers and the 'through' colour numbers if necessary. For example the leeks go from green to white but through a yellowy green. The mackerel from black to white but through a grey-blue and a greyish green!

Don't forget to include notes on your impressions of translucency. Try to develop a sense of whether the translucency goes all the way through or if there's a surface skin which is more ... or less opaque.

Remember some foods change their colour and translucency when they are cooked. For example an egg (both in and out of it's shell) will become more opaque when cooked and a piece of asparagus cooked will become brighter deeper coloured and more translucent. Melted butter is translucent as is warm liquid honey whereas the chilled versions of both are much more opaque.

Keep notes on this. For example do you think something may be 95% translucent like an orange or a grape. Maybe 75% translucent, (a raspberry) maybe 2/3rds translucent (white fish meat fat etc.) or half translucent or less. Keep notes on your impressions of this too.
See translucency p60.

The way you use this information will depend on the properties of your preferred clay.

It may be that the inspiration, or the time to do it comes first and out of season, and you have no notes to work from. In this case you have little alternative but to work from photographs. If this is the case I advise getting several photographs of the same item and look for those which are taken on a white background because the balance of colour is more likely to be correct. Then you only have to worry about the light source. *See colour and light and metamerism p56.*

Every year my visit to the Paris SIMP miniatures fair comes with a trip to an art shop on Quai Voltaire to pick up my favourite pastels. On the way home this year, dropping into a small supermarket I came upon these intensely purple, tiny little turnips. And huge purple fresh 'Elephant' garlic. Of course I couldn't

Pinning down the Purple in Paris
A sketch made with pastels

make the scene there, nor take the garlic home, or even fix the colours in any other way. Nothing could be done except to take a sketch then and there in my hotel room. I called this process 'Pinning down the Purple in Paris' ... a little 'in joke' as we also took a meal in a very purple restaurant. But that's another story ...

If you have time, it's great to make your colour mix experiments then and there, coming out with something like these.

See p21 for garlic recipes.

Turnip purple recipe In Premo
Magenta : Purple : Pomegranate 2:2:1

Turnip purple recipe In Kato
Magenta:Violet:Black
16:16:1

Turnip Purple In Kato
Violet : Red 1:1

Almond Green In Kato
Basic Summer Leaf : White 4:1

Turnip purple Pastel cc no 55 and 66 - 16 for top

Almond Green Pastel 51 & 16

Colours pinned down

So, how can you pin down colours effectively every time when you don't have time or interest in making a drawing?

> Broad beans
> "Pod yellow-green 4 on scrapbooking chart, lime zest 2 on Dulux, Edges accents and tip woodland fern 2-3 on Dulux or green 6 on scrapbooking chart
> Collar Tarragon glory 1 or green 8 on scrapbooking wheel Lined with fluffy white!
> Beans lime zest 3 with lime zest 2 accents edges and top"

I started out by using Dulux colour charts and also tried a scrapbooking colour wheel given to me by miniatures friend.

Here's how I started:

This method is not perfect because it changes in different lights or hours after the pod is harvested e.g. later in brighter light I re-identified and re-wrote it as "Beans lime zest 6 with lime zest 2-3 highlights, 'Fur'-kiwi burst 6". Obviously this method has other limitations, including the number of variants of colours and also the likelihood of the Dulux company getting very annoyed by hoards of miniaturists storming B&Q to pick up one of every colour chart each.

Another method

And then I thought of how the paint companies themselves identify colours, and not having expensive scanners I went to a 'paint' program on my computer and sampled different areas on the photograph which gave me these results, which gave this rather nice colour box.

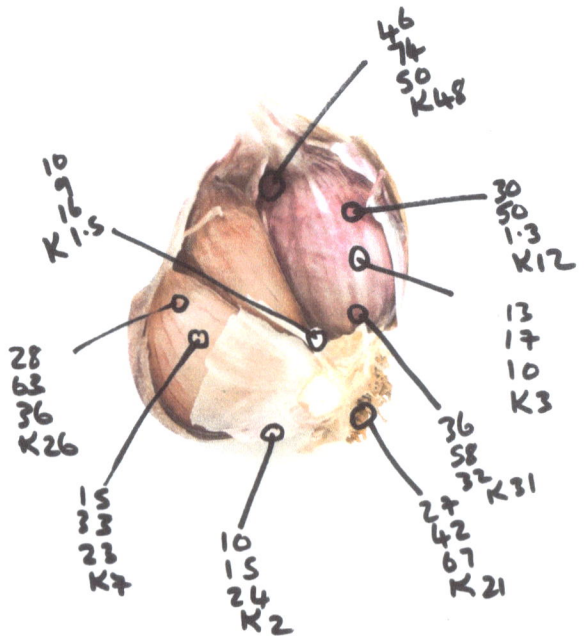

This method also has it's drawbacks. One being that the sample can be flawed and another that however good the photograph, it is still one step away from reality. It is also very laborious and just doesn't feel 'artistic' because the computer replaces your own colour recognition,

And then ...
Then I tried a really good CMYK colour chart and started to identify the colours from the chart. Using these I got the basis of the colours I used in this book. The drawbacks of using this method is that your printer will print out your version of the chart differently to mine. And may print differently on different occasions. But if it's just for your use, and you always use the same chart this method can work really well. Whatever method you prefer, always use the same chart in the same light conditions. Or make different identifications for other light conditions. *See colour and light and metamerism p56.*

Broad Bean Light In Fimo
White : Basic Spring Green : Basic Summer Leaf 10:1:1

Garlic Pink In Fimo
29 Carmine : 23 Bordeaux : Light Grey Base 1:1:4

Professional Tip
Or for a more extensive colour recognition chart I recommend searching "CMYK colour chart", mentioned in the acknowledgements and sources of this book.

Finally ...
To short cut all this hassle, you can take this book out with you to the shops or into the garden or just to your kitchen to write down the colours that you see for later matching.

Another use of a 'pinned down purple' on the left a real cooked octopus. Yes I did have to buy one, and cook it, for this experiment! On the right my miniature version upside down on a food preparation board

"One man's magenta"

So, just a recap about real life colour and clay colour before we dive further into the colours themselves.

It's unfortunately impossible to say with any accuracy that polymer clay colours are fixed and unchanging. Clay companies tweak their mixes all the time and don't always notify their customers of changes so it's important especially if you're embarking on a big project using the recipes described in this book that you check the packet colours correspond with the colour you are expecting to see.

For example if you're working from an old copy of my first book the colour formerly known as 'terracotta' was actually a brown. The clay company has since corrected the error and introduced a true terracotta and renamed the original, more aptly as chocolate. But it's still a slightly different colour, as is the red. That being said my original basic colours list is still valid and much of it is repeated in the centre pages here.

Also don't go by names (or even by numbers) and assume that one brand's version of Magenta will be called Magenta or that one is the same as another brand's. They are not standardised to print colours.

Many colours in different ranges are labelled with the same or similar names. Magenta in one clay is different from a magenta in another range. To check whether the magenta you're using truly is a magenta you could get hold of a pantone swatch (expensive) and look for the real printers magenta, or use a web search. *See p103.* Or look at this box. This is as near a true Magenta as we can make it. Remember that colours can sometimes look less strong although they are the same hue because they are printed on paper which can absorb a lot of the colour or reflect the light in a different way than you expect it to. But a magenta should look pretty much like this. If it doesn't, try to identify in your mind whether it has more blue,

Dragon fruit, real and a piece of cane

or more yellow in it. Maybe it has just a little black added?

If the world was fair, and polymer clay was printers ink, we could mix all the colours from Cyan, Magenta, Yellow and Black (which ought to be a mixture of all, but isn't). Yes, I did try it but rapidly drowned under a mountain of failed experiments. However I can tell you that yellow is probably around ten times less strong than blue and magenta is somewhere in the middle. Following CMYK percentages was not the answer, even when drastically 'tweaked' for it's own shortcomings, and for the different brands of clay. And then tweaked again adding stronger red pigment clays to make up for the shortcomings of magenta. One day I'm sure a more mathematical colourist than me will come up with CMYK formulae. During my experiments I came upon the realisation — my life is too short!

Fimo magenta is a pretty true magenta (with just a little base added.) This means you can use it straight from the pack to make this dragon fruit cane and outer skin. The skin 'spurs' cane is a Skinner-shade of magenta through pale spring green to a light mid green.

The middle is simply translucent with black spots let in, you can use inclusions but it's difficult to get the right size. So I made a cane full of spots. *See p13.*

Garnet Red Pastel 39
Nearest match to Magenta

Straight from the pack magenta for dragon fruit
Fimo, Kato, Premo and Pardo

Figs In Cernit or Dukit
Ruby Red
Hue:Translucent 1:1

Radicchio In Fimo
2 Red : Burgundy
1:1 Hue:Translucent 1:1

Dark Purple In Premo
Alizarin : Ultramarine : Pomegranate 2:1:1 (for garlic)

'Pinky Purple' In Premo
Alizarin : Yellow 1:1 (for garlic)

Pink In Premo
Alizarin : White 2:3 (for garlic)

CHAPTER TWO
Seeing Red

1	2	3
4	5	6
7	8	9

Recipe Key: 1 p58 (Green Bean)   2 p53 (Deep Pink)   3 p53 (Raspberry)

4 p92 (Pastels 67 & 46)   5 p48 Basic Purple   6 p53 (Strawberry)

7 p51 (Burgundy Fimo)   8 p53 (Pink Champagne)   9 p31 (Christmas Red)

Powder and paint uses

Powder colours

Where creating a caned colour would be difficult or unsuccessful e.g. putting a little on the tips of bananas especially where a little subtlety is required.

To put a 'blush' on rosy apples, pomegranates etc. or subtle colour dusting on mushrooms.

To deepen colour and age edges of lettuce or cabbage leaves.

To accentuate edges, as in the suckers of an octopus.

To hide joins between colour and blur edges where a shade jumps too quickly or is impractical because joining the colours is not a natural gradation.

To put a brown cooked look e.g. sweetcorn and griddle lines on fish etc.

To 'dirty' items e.g. potatoes - note the small amount of green on a few potatoes.

The dirty effect can be powders but tea powder can also be used to add an extra 'speckle'. The same ideas can be used on carrots.

The edge of colour changing items like purple edged cabbage, roses etc.

To add a little reality to prevent every fruit/veg etc. looking similar. A little darker orange on some oranges for example.

To add an extra dimension to items which may look a bit flat.

To add a 'bloom' on grapes or leaves which have a white or blue-white bloom. You can use chalks or talcum powder. The finer the powder the better, so a really fine talc is best.

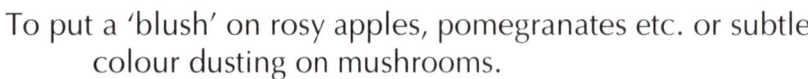
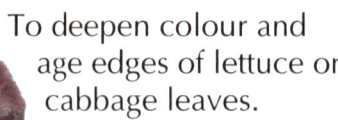

To add sheen, to add gleam/glitter to items with an irregularly reflective surface, e.g. fish scales - see the mackerel project and especially the little sardines. I use cake decorators lustre powders for this but you can also use pearl-ex powders or similar.

I also use pearl-ex metallics on the beetles on p73.

To create 'bleed' e.g. chorizo. For this I use a blend of pure pigment powders (bought from an art shop).

Powders are always applied before baking to allow the pigments to bond with the polymer clay. However to avoid bleed (except when you actually want bleed as above) you should bake as soon as possible, especially when strong pigments are used. See p32.

Wet Paint. Occasionally you need to add paint for a speckled effect, e.g. pears or a mottled or patterned effect e.g. melon skins. Or dipping to create a really subtle thickening e.g. pear, cherry or apple stalks.

Pens can also be used to make small marks spots etc. e.g. pomegranates. Ends of fruits and banana spots. For all of these I would choose a dark brown very fine tipped permanent marker.

Professional Tip

When buying powder colours for nature, my favourite colours are Conte Carres pastel chalks. You can scrape just as much as you need from the chalk making them very easy to use and less likely to spill than tub powders.

Conte Carres come in a huge number of colours. So if you're shopping for them here are my top colours for use in nature representation in polymer clay the first 9 are very close to the basic clay colours as seen in the centre of the book:

Naples yellow 47

violet 55

crimson lake 66

scarlet 28

orange 12

golden yellow 14

St Michaels green 44

Olive green 016

chrome oxide green 75

dark grey green 78

natural Umber 54

red brown 07

Tile 79

Remember not to scrape the number off, you may need it again.

Red is not just red

A strawberry really is not the same colour as a raspberry! Unfortunately when you are first

presented with a box of polymer clay you tend to use the colours you are given and assume a lot about colour based on the colours that appear in front of you. But if you buy a box of strawberries and a box of raspberries and put them side by side you will see that they are completely different colours. With such small fruits, in miniatures it's especially important to differentiate between the two.

So you have to think carefully about your colour mixes in polymer clay. Remember the skin of a strawberry may be a darker colour than the inside when making a cane. I often use some translucent yellow to add to the 'Skinner shade' to lighten and brighten the inside of the strawberry when making this cane.

This difference in different red fruits is even more obvious when you come to making sauce colours with liquid polymer and oil colours for example. A cheap box of oil paints will not give you the basis for either strawberry or raspberry sauce! You really need to look at the standard reds in a cheap paint box. They often don't have the carmine which is better for raspberry. And more often have a red which is towards scarlet and vermilion, even for strawberry sauce this isn't quite right.

Liquid Polymer

Several clay companies now produce a liquid polymer which is really useful for reproducing liquids and very translucent items although it has a few irritating tendencies caused by air bubbles. Air bubbles can adversely affect the translucency. They can also come to the edge of the inside of a mould and cause the surface of the item you are moulding to become 'pitted'. They can also expand when the material is in a container and subsequently baked, causing both the material and the container to crack. This makes them difficult to use as liquids inside glass bottles.

*Strawberry Sauce In Liquid Polymer
Add Scarlet Lake oil paint*

*Raspberry Sauce In Liquid Polymer
Add Alizarin Crimson oil paint*

Professional Tip
Between uses keep Liquid Polymer bottles upside down in a glass or jar to make sure the liquid is always near the tip and help prevent air bubbles forming in moved liquid.

Cherries

These cherries are an extremely simple idea but show how much nicer they look with a mixture of colour mixes.   Cherries are rarely all the same colour!

Stalks

Make up a really well conditioned clay in a basic spring green.

If you can, use a flexible clay for the stalks or add just a little softener like sculpey mould maker. If you don't have a clay gun you'll have to roll tiny strands of clay and pre-cook them.   However it's much easier to get a good result if you have a clay gun (Kemper tools or Makins clay)

Even using the disc with the smallest holes does not produce stalks as thin as we want them. The more delicate your stalks ... the better.   I make it thinner by pulling the

'threads' as they come out of the extruder until they snap off.   Then using the thinnest pieces. BUT leave it to cool and settle a bit after extruding.   It's hard to work with if it's too sticky.

Take a short piece of really thin stalk *before cooking* and fold it over and pinch the end up

a bit. You can also make some single stalks. Remember the length is less important than the thickness at this stage as you can trim it back once it's baked.

Bake all the stalks you want at once.

Dip the very ends of the baked stalks, after baking, in some earth brown paint.   This gives a more realistic effect as long as it's subtle!

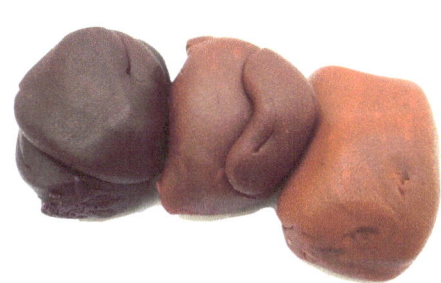

Cherries are, on the face of it a fairly easy fruit to make, However getting the colour and translucency right can be a bit tricky.   It's important you make several shades of colour. I've used Du-kit red, burgundy and black in various proportions for this.

I always advise working from life.   So, if it's cherry season when you're reading this, go and get some!   Otherwise the internet is a good source of photos but watch out for odd lighting castes.

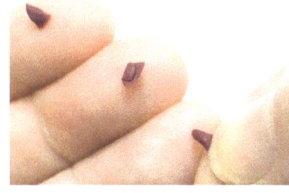

I advise making up as many balls of colour as you can be bothered to do all at once, and then putting the stalks in all of them.

Here's a neat trick for making several balls at once: Roll out a sausage of colour hold it in one hand, across your forefinger, nip a tiny piece off the end with your thumbnail straight on to one of your fingers on the other hand. Do this a couple of times more so you have 3 little bits at once.

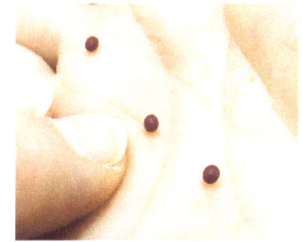

Upturn them onto the palm of your other hand

(the same one that is holding the main piece) and roll them around with the fingers. With a little practise you should be able to both judge the size of piece you need and get them all evenly rolled.

I use Liquid Fimo to make sure the cherries don't drop off the stalks.

Obviously you don't want to fiddle about making more cherries than necessary, so I make a mould from a pile of ball shapes and, if filling cherry bags, push some moulded clay into the bottom of the bag and as far up the side as I think won't be too visible in the final result.

Then, using a little Liquid Fimo as a glue, add a few more little balls of colour before putting a few cherries on stalks at the front to complete the scene.

The brown paper bags are shown on p84. Make 'red' cherries from the two recipes below and mixes of those two recipes.

Cut the stalks to the right size. About 1cm is best. Dip all the ends gently into liquid Fimo. Don't use too much or you'll make a terrible mess!

*Cherry recipe 1 in Premo
Alizarin Crimson : Marine 1:1
Hue:translucent 1:2*

Using a cocktail stick, make holes in the little cherries and push the stalks into them. You may need to hold the stalks apart to get two separate cherries on. If you do feel the need to make the little line down the side of the cherry, make sure this is subtle and you certainly don't need to do all of them as they won't be seen.

*Cherry recipe 2 - use Pomegranate Premo or basic ruby red in other clays.
Hue:Tanslucent 1:4*

*Yellow cherry recipe
Use Fimo golden yellow to white 1:4
Hue:Translucent 1:6
Kato1:1
Hue:Translucent 1:2
Pardo yellow to white 1:3.
Hue:Translucent 1:2*

Dust with Carres colours vermillion 03 and bright red 65

Tomatoes are not the colour I always thought they were!

All the points I've previously made about pinning down the colour to your own satisfaction go double here.   The problem of unnatural colour pigments rears it's ugly head here. *See p38.* Compound this with the problem of some clays being a little too translucent for outer skins *(see p60)* mean that tomatoes are a difficult vegetable (fruit) to get right in polymer clay because of their relative translucency throughout and because 'tomato' is a particular colour which is difficult to 'remember'.   We usually remember them as red.   But red tomatoes are very much over ripe.   Of course, even more than many other fruits their colours vary from under ripe to over ripe and all points in between.   They are also of all sizes and shapes but that would be another book!

When making tomatoes as with any other fruit, you need to consider whether you are making them whole or as a cane or simply whole but with a skin on because this will affect the mix/es that you make.   I think tomatoes need about 70% translucent if you are making whole fruits without a skin. When making a skin it needs to be very fine and much more opaque. Consider making a Skinner-shaded skin with several colours from the grid for Mediterranean tomatoes and also remember the tops of a Mediterranean garden tomato may be badly cracked.   Before I moved to Spain I thought tomatoes were the regular (and rather tasteless) Dutch varieties.   Even in my garden in England the types we grew were predictable colours and shapes with regular formation and pigmentation.   As an artist (and greedy person) I now have a much greater respect for the humble tomato.

Achieving sufficient contrast

This is particularly important in the smaller scales where if contrast is not achieved you will lose all definition and impression of what your miniature is supposed to represent.   Here is an illustration where I used a contrast which would have been sufficient in a cane with only two seed parts.

real tomatoes

But when I cut and re stacked for a Mediterranean style tomato, so that the seeds were even smaller there simply wasn't enough contrast to carry it. How to solve this?

Firstly I would mix the colour from yellow and red clays. But avoiding any clays which have a distinctly fluorescent caste. Unless the colour achieved looks as if it needs a 'lift' in which case there may be an argument for adding colours with optical brighteners.

tomato colours

See p56 colour and light and metamerism.

Outlining and exaggeration

Sounds a bit childish doesn't it? But sometimes to add to the definition between parts of a composition with similar colours you have to outline the edges to improve the definition between sections. Scale miniatures simply will not support a blurred edge between two indistinct colours such as the orangey pink flesh of a tomato and the translucent seed protection part. You simply have to have a slight exaggeration of the edge. In the case of tomatoes, I put a very fine but deep red edge to the seed part.

The seed itself should be very opaque to exaggerate it, and the translucent ... even more translucent. I used to add some red colour to the wet seed 'sheath'. But now I put only translucent or just the slightest stain with a strongly pigmented colour and won't use one of the clays with more opaque filler in for that part because even a small amount simply blurs

Basic tomato colour: see centre pages, add translucent depending on whether making whole tomatoes only or a cane to cut. You can also mix with proportions of the Basic orange or the Basic ruby red for some variation.

Conte Carres 28 & 43 with darker reds plus yellows and greens for details.

the definition. The centre of a caned tomato has a mix of the main colour with white of at least 50/50, this also increases the opacity and defines the centre.

A solid opaque and slightly redder mix is recommended for the skin of a tomato cane. Don't forget tomatoes can sometimes have green sides or tops and even big ugly stained cracks.

Tomato canes appear in full in my books Miniature Challenges Part 1 and Miniature Food Masterclass

Simple Rules for making miniatures from caned clay are

- *Simplify*
- *Exaggerate*
- *Check colour values*
- *Subtle or stronger outlines*

Simplify the design to the most important elements which create the 'essence' of the thing. You can't possibly add every element to something which will be so small in the final object for the polymer to be less than one particle thin. However if a slightly stronger line than is really visible is necessary to make the thing look real add it in and increase its thickness, e.g. gooseberries.

When caning using natures colours one must often cheat a little because the colour values can often have too little contrast between them to be readable when they are reduced. Sometimes you must increase the depth or darkness of the colour at the edge of that element. Try using a darkened version of the actual colour or a brightened version of the lighter colour.

For example in the skin on my onion canes I add dark brown and bright orange side by side to create stronger but still very fine lines. Another 'trick I use is to 'outline' the sharp element ... in this case the line, with translucent. It just makes it possible to make the line finer but still achieve a similar sharpness

These 'cheats' disappear in the tiny onions but are just strong enough to make sure the line is visible.

Other cheats include white lines, black lines or contrasting colour lines around the edges or between elements of a design.

For example my poinsettia canes and my leaf canes contain bright accents to accentuate changes in colour or borders of shapes. This is because red and green or various greens together can be very similar in colour value and also the eye can be confused by red and green together without accents between the colours. The best accents are just exaggerations of reality. So for a poinsettia cane, which is made of two leaf canes one red and one green, I put a very bright pale green line in the veins alongside perhaps a very dark green ... almost black line. This is on both of the two colours.

I also lowlight the edges of the whole leaves with black to make them stand out against

neighbouring leaves. These dark lines are very fine ... but absolutely necessary as I found out the first time I ever made a poinsettia cane!

Other examples where I need to exaggerate a little include autumn leaves.
See p82.

Christmas Red - Premo Pomegranate or Kato Red : Magenta 1:1

Colour 'bleed'

Colour bleed can be a problem. But it can also be an effect that you use deliberately.

Donna Kato does some beautiful face canes where the slight 'bleed' of the black into the pink of the faces causes a beautiful purple 'wash' effect round the design. To achieve this effect you really need to use a lot of translucent in the colour being 'washed' into, and leave the cane for quite a long time as clay manufacturers do try to minimise the bleed as much as possible. But there are other ways of achieving bleed deliberately, and one is to add extra pigment powders to your clay.

Or you can just coat one piece of clay with pigment and allow it to bleed into the next. Actually it will bleed both ways, but if one of your colours is the same colour as the powder it won't show or if one side is a dark colour it will be less visible on that side. Of course your clay needs to be soft and sticky enough to take up the powder and still stick to the next piece. Or you can paint a very thin layer of liquid polymer on and add the powder to that. Be careful doing this though as it can cause elements to 'slip' against each other if either too powdery ... or too liquid.

To make chorizo, which in real life has a 'bleed' of paprika into the fat in the sausage I mix up the main meat colour basic meat colour (or the Jamon mix as on the following page), and the fat colour and leave all together in in small rounded lumps then throw the red pigment (paprika colour) into the whole lot (imitating life) and when the whole cane is squashed together and left for a relatively short time the colour bleed is complete. You can choose the stage at which you feel the bleed into the fat colour is sufficient before you bake. Once baked the bleed is almost completely stopped. I say almost because perhaps there is still an almost imperceptible continuation of the pigment bleed, especially in humid conditions. For the skin I make a translucent and ochre mix 3:1 and put on a very thin skin.

Remember, the results of mixing pigment powders and polymer clays have not been tested and therefore I cannot recommend colours which are safe. As a general rule however colours sold in sugar craft and baking shops are tested to be non-toxic, though no information is available on the effects of baking within polymer clay. For this reason I cannot recommend experimentation except among professionals using a separate oven.

Meat Mix

Chocolate : Red : Foundation Mix 2

1:1:2

Colour checking

Colour checking can be very time consuming. I recently timed how long it takes to mix, bake, check and then mix again for the meat colours for Jamon Iberico (Serrano ham) for example. This is a basic 3 colours plus a couple of extra 'tweaks' for subtle variations. It took a whole morning. Around 3 hours. That's not an insignificant investment in time, but it has to be done if you want a predictable result. Of course, if you're making regular large quantities of the same colour mix and you're using the same batch of clay, you can pretty much rely on your recipe. But any changes of type of clay or even widely distinct batches may throw up surprising and annoying results if you don't check. And any recipe you write down will be useful as a starting point for future mixes. You can't rely on how an unbaked clay looks either, especially when using a large proportion of translucent. The translucent tends to whiten unbaked clay. The real result can only be seen once the materials which are fairly opaque when unbaked become translucent when polymerised. This can lead to a colour looking significantly darker after baking. This is not what's called 'colour shift'. It's merely the effect of unbaked translucent.

At the end of this experiment (using Fimo) I decided to use basic meat mix plus 10% 'real' red (not shown), with twice as much translucent as in my normal basic meat mix, to take account of what the ham looks like when cut.

And the same basic with red and black and blue added for the very dry meat which is much browner.

This seems to be a good time to mention what I call 'real red'.

'Real red' to me is equal to the old Fimo red, as it was when I started around 25 years ago! Sadly this colour has been discontinued for around 15 of those years and it's by sheer luck that I was offered a large batch a year or so later ... which I snapped up! However, if you're normally a Fimo user, you can substitute by mixing the two Fimo reds in equal proportions with Kato clay's pigment red 1:1:1.

There is a basic meat mix in several brands on p52.

Tip: *when making up any meat cane avoid regular thickness' and over straight lines which would give your work a 'cartoonish' look.*

Lobster colours

I've put the lobster here because this is what a cooked lobster looks like to me. In reality lobsters come in all sorts of colours including blue and black. And there have even been cases of lobsters being exactly half and half blue and red! But leaving aside the weird and wonderful freaks of nature, most people are expecting a lobster on a plate, to look something between orange and teracotta. But within that colour range there are various shades from quite pinky to a red brown colour.

The underneath colour is a creamy colour and if you're making a cane, as I have, you need to make spots. A careful look at the part cane on the right of the illustration shows that I started putting light spots within the dark area and continued by putting dark spots within the light colour built up the shape of the carapace and accentuated the separate parts with a mid brown line. It's almost impossible to make the lines line up perfectly in the mould, however a bit of dusting powder can help fuzz any really obvious misaligns. I used bits of the same cane for the claws. The whiskers are pre-baked from the main colour and the eyes are very small beads. Both whiskers and beads are attached with liquid polymer. I like to attach the whiskers after first bake so that I can drill the holes precisely to accept them.

Pastel 07 red brown and 79 tile for cooked red lobster

Pastel 73 cold green and 42 sepia grey for a blue lobster

Crab In Premo
Angie's Deep Orange Base (p53)

Lobster In Fimo Ochre : Red 3:1
In Premo Alizarin : Cadmium Yellow 1:7

Lobster Belly
Champagne : Pale Translucent Cream 1:1

'Pinky-prawny-salmony' colours

Prawns appeared in my book Making Miniature foods but since then I've updated them by making each line Skinner-shaded. Looking carefully at prawns in my local shops and on internet images there are a few different kind of pinks in cooked prawns, so don't get too hung up on the shade of pink unless you are trying to replicate a particular breed of prawns from a particular area. I did notice that the darker colour was usually near the outer edge of each section of the shell

so I've reversed the direction of the shading by simply turning the original stack upside down and adding the light slice on the other side. This is barely noticeable. But I am a bit of a perfectionist and when I find I've been making even a tiny mistake like this for years, it really annoys me!

You can also add a little extra subtle touch by using powder on the edge before rolling the prawn. This can make them look grilled. If you have endless time for your hobby, making legs can be fiddly ... but fun to look at. Make sure you put the legs on before you curl the prawn shape. Otherwise it's almost impossible.

Salmon
Angie's Deep Orange Base : Translucent 1:10

Prawns
Salmon mix as above : White 1:1
Shade to Flesh Pink

Prawn, salmon & lobster colours

CHAPTER THREE
Mellow Yellow

1	2	3
4	5	6
7	8	9

Recipe Key: 1 p45 (Solid Butter)   2 p48 Basic Orange   3 p44 (Pineapple)

4 p52 (Carrot)   5 p48 Golden Yellow   6 p19 (Broad Bean Light)

7 p45 (Banana)   8 p39 (Orange Marrow)   9 p51 (Premo Ecru)

Pigment problems

When is an orange not an orange? When it's a polymer clay orange pigment!

One of the worst offenders in my

Real oranges and packets of clay

'unrealistic pigments' - least wanted - list is orange, and this seems to be a problem throughout all ranges. I see little likelihood of these colours being corrected to be more natural as they are most probably better loved by jewellery artists.

BUT these colours are often close to carrot colour.

However a better recipe for carrot is on p52. The centre of a carrot is often slightly more white and more translucent. Here I've put some of the patterns (exaggerated) in the cane although these will be almost invisible in the miniature version - I believe if you can ... you should. Just imagine someone is going to take a magnifying glass to your work and you won't go too far wrong!

There are many many varieties of mandarins satsumas, tangerines and the like but I'm using tangerine as a catch all for the darker skinned varieties of the type. For the lighter skinned ones use the orange recipes below.

Oranges dark and light Use basic orange and mix of basic orange and basic golden yellow. Depending on brand use up to 50% translucent to 'lighten' the density of the colour for miniatures.

Pumpkin Halloween type - Skin = Basic orange + Basic tomato+ White 1:1:1 Flesh = 1:3 colour to translucent

Orange Pith - Use Basic Pale Cream and add more white if needed

Carrot Finish

Use Conte Leaf Green 76 to powder stalk end and some tea powder for dirt.

Real carrot and cane

Fluorescence in orange packet clays

When I came to take pictures of the orange packet clays, I thought, actually they don't look as bad as I always thought. What on earth is going on? Are my eyes playing tricks on me? Sure they looked a teeny bit garish. But all in all they matched pretty well ... in daylight photography. But when I went back to pack away the colours as the sun was going down (losing some of it's spectrum) suddenly there it was. That awful fluorescence! Just starting to appear ... but definitely there! But It still didn't show up to be as garish on my camera as it did in real life. This whole problem is covered in more detail in the 'Colour and light' and 'Metamerism' section of my book on page 56 of this book.

Mixing it up!

I used to think that I had to choose one brand of clay and stay with it out of loyalty ... or because the clays were not inter mixable. The idea that the clays are not inter mixable is almost like an urban myth. Even the adult versions of the clay in most countries have to be non-toxic if swallowed by children. Please note that this isn't always the case and you should **NEVER** allow your young child to swallow polymer clay or to play with it unsupervised. And you shouldn't encourage your children to intermix clays just to be on the safe side.

However, as a grown up artist I experiment with mixing clays. For legal reasons I'm not recommending that you do, but in the interests of openness I admit I often mix clays in my work.

Yellow Marrow

Golden Yellow : Red 100:1

Hue:Trans 4:6

Orange Marrow In Fimo

Lemon Yellow : Carmine 30:1

Hue:Trans 4:6

Ageing and presentation

When planning to make your miniature scene, you need to be aware of the setting and of the 'freshness' of your produce. Although this in a garden scene so it's up to the maker to present the choice. Some varieties of marrows for example come in from the garden one

Comparison between freshly harvested marrows and the same ones a month or two later. Some change colour slightly. Some dramatically.

applies to all the 'products' mentioned in this book it applies most to fruit and vegetables. This can affect the colour a good deal. A garden cauliflower is not going to look anything like a fresh shop cauliflower which in turn is not going to look anything like one which has been left to wilt and go a bit brown in the kitchen.

A collector may well only think about this after he or she has put a trimmed cauliflower

Real marrow and cane

the cane appears lighter because of the translucent clay being uncooked

colour but would never be eaten until they have matured in store. This picture shows the difference in colour as it develops over a month or two in the exact same marrows of three different varieties. Notice also how the cut stem changes. So a Christmas storehouse scene will look subtly different from a harvest scene.

For marrow seeds you can use un-roasted sesame seeds as miniature squash seeds, make sure you coat them in some way to keep it from being interesting to 'critters'.

'Turning' leaves for the marrow plant

These colours could have been in the browns with the autumn leaves but I decided to keep them in the yellows because they arrive in my garden in the high summer of late August when the edges of the mature marrow plants are starting to turn. Sometimes the leaves also get a greyish bloom (a fungus I suppose) on them too at this time. To replicate the 'turning ochre of the leaves I mix a Skinner-shaded roll from ochre through to brown and then insert a rough half circle into parts of the leaves or on other parts just a tip of ochre and/or brown. The rest of the leaf is built up very much like one of my cabbage leaves though a bit more subtle. And in this leaf I also added the first spots of the 'bloom' I mentioned. Of course not all leaves on a plant have the dried edges, so I simply cut out smaller leaves from larger leaf slices.

Then I attach the leaves to the side stems. And bake them with the leaf top bent back. The leaves are veined of course.

The marrow base stems are made by extrusion with a clay gun with a hole corer. I wire the base stems with flower wire, and pull one end a little thinner zigzag the whole length leaving the thickest end bent down so it can look as if it grows out of the ground, before attaching the side leaves the base stem with my 'goo' mentioned in garden greens on p64, this has to be supported all the while on folded craft paper.

Professional Tip
Here's a simple neat little trick for this. There are some little cutters around that look like marrow leaves, and you can alter them with pliers to be more of the shape you want. Altering the size of the cut leaf using the same cutter simply by cutting a leaf out once and then moving the cutter sideways or lengthwise slightly over the same leaf and cutting again, effectively either narrowing or shortening the leaf ... or both. The shape will be altered a little but you can use your fingers gently to 'tweak' bits back into shape.

My pre-baked marrows, tendrils and marrow flowers are also attached with 'goo' at this stage and the whole thing is baked again. The flowers appear in the following pages.

Designing your cane

Example pumpkin/cucurbit flower notes.

Steps: Select item/s - select the biggest example of that item that you can find - photograph, draw and/or paint the whole item from several angles. Try to imagine you are actually making it and imagine what you will have to re-check.

Measure and write down size or photograph item with measuring tape in situ.

Colour match main colour and either: select/mix the clay then and there, bag and label if doing another day, or simply write down matched colour as it appears on your 'swatch'.

You could of course use "p48 position 1 of colour book exactly matches" … if indeed it does! If you can't find an exact colour mix try to make notes to give you a fighting chance of getting as near as possible

Don't forget to colour match any additional colours. Don't spoil a project by using a perfect yellow … but the wrong green!

Don't forget to make notes about translucency

I make notes about the light I took the pics or made the colour recognition in too. The date is there to match seasonality, in case you're a purist. It's no good for instance making a garden scene that has marrows and winter broccoli in at the same time. Unless of course you want to throw those rules out of the window as I do, and make a magical garden where everything is in season at the same time!

> e.g. "Cucurbit flower up to 7" across"
>
> Dukit Golden yellow = perfect match inc translucency.
> Extremely saturated colour
>
> like Premo cadmium yellow … but just a touch more orangey
>
> cucurbit flower approx 50% translucent
>
> Very sunny day! 29 July

Make additional notes

You could also add the colour and length of the pistil. I forgot that at the time of taking my notes. Fortunately my pictures came out very well.

Note petal shapes, formation of veining to petals etc.

5 petals in trumpet shape

3 parallel, light spring green veins visible on outside of each petal. Central = longest, only central vein visible on inside. Green ring round central pistil.

The 5 pointed flower cutter shape was put on to mark the place to insert the green lines as 5 is a difficult number to divide into by eye. The same cutter is used to cut flower shapes from thin slices of the cane.

Fine flower petals using the cut and cross method

In this demonstration I'm just making an extremely simple yellow flower for a tomato plant. I use the same method for little white flowers for peppers. This also works for tiny calyxes for tomatoes and strawberries etc.

Cut a long thin strip of your clay the depth of the petal you want (or a little wider) and the width of the diameter of the flower approximately. Cut the edge of the strip diagonally. This will give your petals a fine tip.

If you have a flower back mould (that's the part of the flower called the receptacle and the calyx) fill it with green clay, if you don't have a mould just make a small blob on a stalk (like an upside down teardrop shape) and press an indentation into it with a ball tool.

Cut very fine slices with a single sided blade. If you can get the clay to leave the blade (and there's a trick to this too!) you should. The trick for removing the clay from the blade is to cut and scrape towards you on the tile in one motion. Then turn the angle of the blade so that the top is slightly towards you and push

real tomato flowers

back to scrape it off the blade. Then cut the next piece and continue until you have built up a line or more than one line of quite a few on your tile. This makes it quicker to assemble the flowers later. If the petal clings to the blade, place it directly on to the clay in the mould, using the stickiness of the clay to pull the petal off. Be careful with the blade!

Assemble by sticking 3 petals crossing in the middle using a cocktail stick to pick the petals up by swiping with a sideways motion, and, if making a tomato flower you will need to make a small pistil to sit in in the centre. Then squeeze the mould until the flower comes away. Usually the flower will come out reasonably easily. But maybe occasionally it will stick. Then you need to squeeze really hard and just expect to squash that flower.

When I have a lot of flowers I bake them and add then to a plant later with green 'goo'

See p64.

If you want your petals even more delicate and a bit curved, with a bit of practise you can press them with a ball tool onto a piece of EVA sponge before adding them to the clay in the mould. But this can be a bit fiddly!

Yellow recipes

Most of these mixes use basic golden yellow or pale translucent cream or both and many of the colours mix down from the previous ones. Since all of them call for very subtle touches of colour you should always add just a touch at a time until the desired colour is achieved, and, because the baking process tends to darken any semi translucent colours try mixing one shade lighter first. You can always add extra colour, but you can't take it away.

This is one of those times when you can't get away with a slightly wrong colour. There's only so far maturing will take a cheese!

Pineapple Colour
Basic Golden Yellow : Basic Tomato Red
100:1
Hue:Translucent 1:20

For the lines in a pineapple
White : Translucent 1:1 with just a little of the main mix added to take the 'bright whiteness' off.

Butter and cheese.

Making butter in polymer clay for miniature or full size imitation projects is really quite a simple recipe. It's one of the things I use leftovers for: leftover pineapple mix.

To make butter in various stages.

Partially melted butter is half way between the two recipes above.

Pale Yellow Cheese base recipe (brie centre etc.). Note this mix uses leftovers!

'Melted' Butter
Pineapple Colour (p44) plus liquid polymer

'Solid' Butter
Pineapple colour : White
1:4

Translucent Cheese Mix
Use Pale Translucent Cream and add scraps of flesh colour clay and orange or extra white, a little at a time, until you get just the colour you need. Remember the 'melty' centre of ripe Camembert will have more translucent and a little more colour.

Banana Colour
Golden Yellow : Champagne : FC2
1:3:2 For maize /
sweetcorn add translucent

Pastels for BBQ 18 & 80

Buttery Yellow Potatoes
Foundation Colour 2 :
left over pineapple mix : ochre
50:5:1

Asparagus Yellow In Fimo
Pale Cream Mix : Yellow
6:1

CHAPTER FOUR
Colour Pages

1	2	3
4	5	6
7	8	9

All mixes are on the following 2 pages Basic Colour Recipes, for all clays where possible.

Basic Colour Recipe	Dukit Mixed by Paul Currie	Premo Mixed by Angie Scarr	Cernit Mixed by Karen Walker
Basic Pale Cream	02 White 10 Cream Base 1 (02 White 16 40 Yellow 3 30 Orange 1)	White 100 Translucent 20 Cadmium yellow 3 Sunshine 1	027 Opaque White 50 700 Yellow 1
Basic Purple	90 Ruby 8 80 Violet 1 02 White 1	Magenta 2 Purple 2 Pomegranate 1	900 Purple 7 463 Xmas Red 2 027 Opaque White 1
Basic Ruby Red	10 Red 16 90 Ruby 1 02 White 4	Pomegranate (as-is)	420 Carmine Red 100 900 Purple 1
Basic Tomato Red	20 Scarlet 6 30 Orange 10 02 White 1	Cadmium red 1 Cadmium yellow 5	700 Yellow 3 428 Poppy Red 2
Basic Orange	30 Orange 3 02 White 2 40 Yellow 1	Cadmium red 2 Cadmium yellow 100	700 Yellow 20 428 Poppy Red 1
Basic Golden Yellow	40 Yellow 80 10 Red 1 02 White 32	Cadmium yellow 100 Magenta 1	062 Yellow 9 056 Orange 1
Basic Spring Green	45 Lemon 12 240 Fluoro Yellow 12 51 Leaf Green 1 02 White 2	Wasabi 10 Cadmium yellow 5 Marine 1	611 Light Green 2 027 Opaque White 1 700 Yellow 2
Basic Summer Leaf	51 Leaf Green 4 40 Yellow 8 01 Black 1 02 White 1	Ultramarine 3 Cadmium yellow 10	611 Light Green 10 645 Olive 9 027 Opaque White 1
Basic Darkest Leaf Green	53 Green 1 40 Yellow 3 01 Black 2	Ultramarine 4 Cadmium yellow 10 Black 7	645 Olive

Some colour mixes have been "optimised" to provide readable numbers, while not changing the recipe significantly. Use colours between these basic colours to add variety to your mixes. Try mixing down with white, grey, ecru, cream and of course translucent. Some suggested mixes are shown on the following pages.

Kato Mixed by Tony Aquino	Pardo Mixed by Angie Scarr	Fimo Mixed by Angie Scarr	Basic Colour Recipe
White 100 Cream Base 1 (Yellow 10 Brown 1)	100 White 50 200 Yellow 1	0 White 100 02 Champagne 5 1 Yellow 1	Basic Pale Cream
Magenta 15 Violet 10 Red 2	601 Cyan 1 501 Magenta 10 200 Yellow 3	29 Red 1 21 Magenta 1 33 Blue 1	Basic Purple
Red 6 Magenta 6 White 1	400 Red 4 501 Magenta 1	29 Red 1 21 Magenta 1	Basic Ruby Red
Orange 7 Red 1 White 1	400 Red 1 200 Yellow 4	1 Yellow 1 2 Red 1	Basic Tomato Red
Yellow 12 White 3 Orange 3 Brown 1	501 Magenta 1 200 Yellow 20	1 Yellow 10 2 Red 1	Basic Orange
Yellow 17 Gold Base 3 (White 75 Green 25 Brown 6)	200 Yellow 100 501 Magenta 1	1 Yellow 20 21 Magenta 1	Basic Golden Yellow
Yellow 60 White 15 Green 5 Brown 4	601 Cyan 1 200 Yellow 20	33 Blue 1 1 Yellow 10	Basic Spring Green
Yellow 14 White 2 Green 7 Brown 12	Mix Not Yet Found - see internet updates	34 Navy 2 15 G Yellow 10 57 Leaf Gr 10	Basic Summer Leaf
Green 10 Brown 8 Black 1	Mix Not Yet Found - see internet updates	9 Black 2 34 Navy 4 15 G Yellow 10	Basic Darkest Leaf Green

NB. The greens were recognised in full Spanish summer sun, for indoor display you may need to add extra blue and even a little black for the darker colour. Due to printing processes colours given to the clay companies may not have appeared exactly as they do on this page. I personally would leave out the white on Kato and Dukit colour mixes.

Foundation Colour Mixes	Fimo, Premo, Dukit	Kato	Cernit	Pardo
Foundation Mix 1 (FC1)	White to Translucent 1:1	White to Translucent 1:2	White to Translucent 2:1	White to Translucent 2:1
Foundation Mix 2 (FC2)	White to Translucent 1:3 (or use Fimo Doll Porcelain)	White to Translucent 1:6	White to Translucent 2:3 or use Porcelain (as-is)	White to Translucent 2:3 or use Porcelain (as-is)
Cream Mix	Fimo: FC1 to Ochre 40:1 Premo: use ochre mix opposite	FC1 to Ochre 40:1	FC1 to Ochre 40:1	FC1 to Ochre 40:1
Translucent Cream Mix	Fimo: FC2 to Ochre 40:1 Premo: use ochre mix opposite	FC2 to Ochre 40:1	FC2 to Ochre 40:1	FC2 to Ochre 40:1
Pale Cream Mix	Fimo: FC1, Champagne, yellow 40:5:1 Premo: use champagne mix opposite	FC1, Champagne, yellow 40:5:1	FC1, Champagne, yellow 40:5:1	FC1, Champagne, yellow 40:5:1
Pale Translucent Cream Mix	Fimo: FC2, Champagne, yellow 40:5:1 Premo: use champagne mix opposite	FC2, Champagne, yellow 40:5:1	FC2, Champagne, yellow 40:5:1	FC2, Champagne, yellow 40:5:1

If you don't have sensitive scales and you find difficulty matching the largest numbers with the smallest, take 1 in a 100 to be "a scrap". Add bit by bit the smallest amount possible.

Brand Colours Mixed	In Other Brands	
Fimo Ochre In Premo Cad Yellow : Orange : Raw Sienna : White 5:2:1:1	Fimo Ochre In Kato Brown : Basic Golden Yellow : Yellow Pigment Block : White 3:2:1:1	Fimo Ochre In Cernit Yellow : Brown : White 5:1:1
Premo Ecru In Fimo Champagne : Ochre 5:1	Fimo Ecru In Kato White : Yellow : Brown 5:4:4	Premo Ecru In Cernit White : Caramel : Ochre Mix (above) 5:1:1
Fimo Champagne In Premo Ecru : White 3:1	Fimo Champagne In Kato White : Brown : Yellow 10:5:4	Fimo Champagne In Cernit White : Caramel : Ochre Mix (above) 12:1:1
Premo Olive In Fimo Basic Dark Green : Ochre : Light Grey Base 2:2:3	Premo Olive In Kato Basic Summer Leaf : Brown 4:1	Premo Olive In Cernit Olive : White 1:1
Premo Jungle In Fimo Mid Green : Navy : Dark Grey Base 2:1:1	Premo Jungle In Cernit Olive : Pine : Black : White 3:2:1:1	Premo Jungle In Pardo Yellow : Cyan : Black 25:4:4
Premo Sienna In Fimo Mid Green : Terracotta : Chocolate 3:2:2	Premo Sienna In Kato Brown : Orange 10:1	Premo Sienna In Cernit Brown : Black 10:1
Premo Burnt Umber In Fimo Chocolate : Black : Terracotta 8:1:1	Premo Burnt Umber In Kato Brown : Yellow Pigment Block : Black : Red Pigment Block 10:4:2:1	Premo Burnt Umber In Cernit Brown : Basic Summer Leaf : Black 10:1:1
Fimo Terracotta In Cernit 839 Brown : Basic Orange 1:1	Fimo Terracotta In Premo Alizarin Crimson : Cadmium Yellow 1:7	Fimo Terracotta In Kato Cyan : Magenta : Yellow 1:6:15
Fimo Burgundy In Premo Aliziarin Red : Cadmium Yellow 3:1	Fimo Burgundy In Kato Violet : Red Pigment Block 1:1 or Violet : Red 1:2	Fimo Burgundy In Cernit Xmas Red : Blue 10:1

Because of different densities of pigments my brand colour copy mixes may not react in mixdowns with black or white exactly as the original clay.

Angie's Mixdowns

Walnut In Fimo Ochre : Light Grey Base : Teracotta 10:4:1	Walnut In Premo Basic Orange : Raw Sienna : White 2:1:1	Walnut In Kato Brown : Light Grey Base : Yellow 5:1:1
Lavender Green In Fimo 57 Leaf Green : Light Grey Base 1:1	Lavender Green In Premo Olive : Jungle : Light Grey Base 1:1:1	Lavender Green In Cernit Basic Summer Leaf : Light Grey Base 1:2
Basic Meat Mix In Fimo 77 Chocolate : 2 Red : FC2 1:1:2	Basic Meat Mix In Premo Pomegranate : Burnt Umber : FC2 1:1:2	Basic Meat Mix In Kato Burnt Umber Mix (p51) : Red : Red Pigment Block : FC2 2:2:1:4
Dry Sage Green In Fimo Basic Summer Leaf : Champagne : Light Grey Base 1:4:4 For dry sage, green rocks	Dry Sage In Premo Olive : Rhine 1:2	Dry Sage In Cernit Basic Summer Leaf : Caramel : Light Grey Base 1:2:2
Almond Green In Fimo White : Basic Summer Leaf : Basic Spring Green 8:2:1	Almond Green In Premo Basic Summer Green : Light Grey Base 1:1	Almond Green In Cernit Basic Spring Green : Basic Summer Leaf : Light Grey Base 2:1:2
X Bright Green (additive) In Fimo Basic Spring Green : 57 Leaf Green : 37 Blue 30:15:1 Hue : Translucent 1:10 (kiwi)	X Bright Green (additive) In Premo Wasabi : Ultramarine 20:3 Hue : Translucent 1:10 (kiwi)	X Bright Green (additive) In Cernit Basic Spring Green : Basic Summer Leaf : Green 6:2:1
Carrot In Fimo Basic Orange : Basic Tomato : White 8:4:1 Hue : Translucent 4:6	Carrot In Premo Basic Orange : Basic Tomato : White 8:4:1	Carrot In Kato Magenta : Yellow : White 4:10:1
Banana/Maize In Fimo Golden Yellow : Champagne : FC2 1:3:2 For maize / sweetcorn add translucent	Banana / Maize In Premo Cadmium Yellow : Champagne Mix (p51): FC2 1:3:2 For maize / sweetcorn add translucent	Banana / Maize In Cernit Yellow : Champagne Mix (p51): FC2 1:3:2 For maize / sweetcorn add translucent

More of Angie's Favourite Clay Mixes

Rose In Premo Alizarin Crimson : Yellow : Ecru : White 1:1:3:3	Pale Rose In Premo Alizarin Crimson : Yellow : Ecru : White 1:1:6:10	Halloween Pumpkin Basic Orange : Basic Tomato : White 1:1:1 Flesh Hue:Trans 1:3
Deep Pink In Fimo Red : Violet : White 16:1:8	Deep Pink In Cernit Cadmium Red : Light Grey Base 2:1	Angie's Deep Orange Base In Fimo Terracotta : Red 2:1
Angie's Deep Orange Base In Premo Alizarin Crimson : Pomegranate : Cadmium Yellow 1:1:7	"Pink Champagne" In Premo Angie's Deep Orange Base : White 1:1 For unripe cherries & raspberries	"Powder Puff Pink" In Premo Angie's Deep Orange Base : White 1:4
Forget Me Not Blue In Premo White : Ultramarine : Turquoise 10:2:1	Sky Blue In Premo Whie : Turquoise : Ultramarine 10:4:1	Mid Blue In Premo Whie : Turquoise : Ultramarine 1:1:1
Very Pale Green (Broad Beans) In Fimo Basic Summer Leaf : White 1:4	Apple Skin In Fimo Basic Summer Green : White 4:1 For apples & green tomatoes.	Apple Skin In Premo Basic Summer Leaf : White 4:1
Lavender Flowers In Fimo Lilac : White 4:1	Strawberry use Basic Tomato Red Hue:Trans 1:1	Raspberry use Basic Ruby Red Hue:Trans 1:3
"Bluey Leaf Surface" In Premo Jungle : White 1:1 (over mid & dark leaffor brassicas)	"Interesting" Leaf Green Mix In Fimo 57 Leaf Green : Ochre 1:1	Bright Olive In Fimo Basic Summer Leaf : Basic Orange 1:1
Fimo lilac in Premo Purple : White : Ultramarine 3:1:1	Light Caramel In Fimo 77 Chocolate : 0 White 1:2	Chocolate Milk In Fimo 77 Chocolate : 0 White : 9 Black 3:20:1

For other mixes see the website www.angiescarr.co.uk/colourbook

CHAPTER FIVE
Green

Recipe Key:
1 p48 Darkest Leaf
2 p48 Summer & Dark
3 p51 (Premo Jungle)
4 p48 Spring
5 p45 (Banana)
6 p52 (Sage Green)
7 p48 Summer
8 p53 (Bright Olive)
9 p48 Spring & a little Dark

Word for the Day 'Metamerism'

Colour and light - the mind bending bit!

Colour is light reflected from the surface of the object which you are looking at. This reflection is affected by several conditions and this makes the selection of colour for a project really difficult.

Here is a basic problem for you to think about.

As a polymer clay artist or miniaturist trying to re-create a scene with absolute realism, you have to see each colour and match it with a clay. But the clay pigments reflect light differently under differing light conditions and there are several different types of light source. This is called 'metamerism'. Some colour pigments suffer from it more than others. Here's a real life extreme case. I bought a mushroomy brown face flannel, for my mushroom coloured bathroom wall only to find it was greenish in daylight ! Not a problem in this case because it's place was always in the bathroom.

Think about how an item you might want to reproduce may alter its appearance in different lights.

Compound this with the 6 main clay pigment compositions (brands).

Next think about where your work is going to be displayed. Because where it's displayed will have a light source of it's own.

The maths: or is it physics?

So, why does this problem happen? Let's take for example 1 leaf out of the several you could choose in your garden.

Multiply that leaf by the number of lights you can see it in and then by the number of possible lights your work will be displayed in. This is just the formula for the number of ways you might identify the colour you want to simulate.

Then think about the colours available to you, (after choosing your brand or combination of brands of course) and the possible ways

The right hand colour was identified and mixed for the leaf in bright daylight. The colour on the extreme left is the same leaf colour identified and copied in artificial light. I settled on the mid colour, a mix of the two. The picture, by the way was taken in diffused, indoor daylight which was the best light to photograph the difference because the photograph in daylight was right for the right hand colour, energy saver bulbs were right for the left hand colour. As you can see none are quite right in diffused daylight. But the colour I chose was a compromise which looked 'ok' though, unfortunately, I couldn't find a mix that worked in every light.

I chose a leaf as an example because it seems to me that green has the greatest colour shift problem under different lights.

of mixing them.   For example do you mix from pure colours following an RGB (red green and blue) scheme as we did at school with our paints and plasticine, or the CMYK (Cyan Magenta Yellow and black) scheme that printers use.   Or do you mix from already partly mixed down colours presented to us by the colourists in the brand HQs?

Then think about whether the light you're mixing in is the same light your work will be displayed in, or whether you need a formula in front of you for the difference.   Lets call that the colour shift formula.   Will the 'colour shift' formula be the same or different for the other leaves in your garden or the other elements in your composition?

No wonder Van Gogh went crazy!

When you have glued your head back together after all that and think you have an idea of the colour mix you might be aiming for, add to all of that the translucency and surface treatment and how all that will be 'reflected' (pun intended) in photographs of your work.

This is all just a bit too much but does go some way to explain why the 'science' of colour mixing polymer clay is a long way from exact.

Metamerism

So, if this metamerism is so important, why doesn't it get mentioned in other books on polymer clay mixing like the many wonderful recent books on colour mixing for jewellery and art designs?   Put quite simply, if you're designing a wonderful piece of art or jewellery, maybe you'll notice a slight change in colour balance.   A jumping out of some colours under some conditions.   But you're not going to notice in an abstract piece that a colour doesn't match in the same way as you will when you're working from a piece of nature who's pigmentation may also appear different in a different light.   The pigments are chemistry.   The light is physics.

Where metamerism does get mentioned is in industries which produce camouflage where light conditions can make the difference between life and death or in car repair shops where the paint colour could look different under street lights.   It may also make the difference to whether your faithful reproduction of nature in polymer clay, which you may have done in daylight, looks right under the lights of an exhibition hall.

To be fair to the polymer clay companies, how can we blame a chemist working in Northern Europe for coming up with a different mix of chemical pigments to represent the colour 'leaf green', or 'orange', when he's working in a laboratory outside the hours of daylight in winter, from that chosen by a different chemist in a lab in full sun in California for example ... and vice versa.

When I moved to Spain, I thought the light would improve my work ... and actually found my colour work suffered and initially I was very confused as to why.

I don't want you to get too bogged down in this, but I hope it will explain to you, as it did to me.

And you can make your own decision as to how much weight you give this problem in your work.   If it becomes a little too challenging a problem for you read the words of a respected collector on p100.

Colour and light

So, how do you choose a light to work by? Or rather, how do you choose a light to observe by, to mix by, to photograph by and to display by? Ideally those lights should all be the same. But they can't be because you can never tell where your work will be displayed or photographed after it has left your hands and gone into someone else's collection. So your choice is between going with your favourite and sticking to it, or going by your display lights or to the most frequently used customer's light and sticking with that. Or you can go with the widest possible spectrum of light hoping that will cover most bases.

And what is the broadest spectrum light available anyway?

Sadly it's the incandescent bulb which is almost impossible to buy these days. It's wave graph looks almost identical to sunlight

However halogen 'full spectrum' light bulbs are available which according to The Lighting Research Center (LRC)

"usually provide radiant power throughout the visible spectrum, subtle differences in the spectral reflectance characteristics of different objects are discernible. So, when colour identification is part of the visual task, such as for graphic arts, museums and colour printing applications, full-spectrum light sources will ensure good colour discrimination".

You have to remember that any light source which emits a full spectrum will be more costly to run and emit more heat than a standard energy saver or fluorescent bulb. And some may produce UV lights which can in time damage your work. Halogen artwork lights which are specifically designed to protect valuable pieces for Museums and galleries can be costly. Cheaper are fluorescent Artwork Lights which, if your artwork is encased and protected can work well due to the brightness and clarity of their light.

The Fimo green experiments ... results

First I decided on a ratio of 1-10 of the chosen blue with the chosen yellow, and mixed each blue with each yellow to see which produced the most realistic leaf colours. I found blue 37 didn't give any realistic leaf colours with either of the Fimo yellows.

Blue 33 gave realistic colours in the spring green range

And navy blue 34 gave realistic colours in the mid green range. Remembering that navy blue is really just ultramarine with added black I played around with adding more navy and more black for the darker greens.

All these colours were more realistic than Fimo's leaf green which in Mediterranean light looks dull.

Later (and not shown) I played with adding more navy blue and white for the piney greens and the 'dusty' greens such as lavender green.

Green Bean Leaf
Basic Darkest Leaf : Basic Summer Leaf 1:1
underside Basic Spring Green
or follow instructions p64

Green Beans In Fimo
15 Golden Yellow : 34 Navy Blue : 0 White
10:1:1

Broad Bean Pod
Basic Summer Leaf : Basic Spring Green : White : Trans 2:2:1:1

After experimenting with a guessed rato of 1:10 based on experience of yellows to the blues, I found the greens mixed with turquoise had nothing to add to the colour mixes I needed, but did produce an interesting brightening of Fimos leaf green mix.   They may help boost colours in certain artificial lights.

A good "rule of thumb" for greens would be: if mixing for display in standard energy saver artificial light, it is the blue light that's debilitated. Because of this adding more blue will correct the colour towards one which looks more natural in artificial light.

Of course these are just MY perceptions of colour in my location at my age with my garden produce.   Any changes in any of these variables might produce a different result,

I even wonder sometimes if my own eyes might perceive colours differently depending on my mood, my blood pressure, my age.

We should celebrate these differences because in this way all art is defined by the individual artist.

That is why, although I've bowed in this book to the pressure to give recipes, I must stress that your colour matching should be a result of your experience and you shouldn't slavishly follow my recipes which may not work for your eyes or your lighting conditions.   That is why this book gives you the colour strips as possible 'identifiers'.   But you should never be happy with my identification. You should always make your own and just use my mixes as 'hints' if you find yourself completely lost, or if you have a physical problem seeing colour and want a little help.

Dark Marrow Skin
Use Basic Darkest leaf Green in any brand.

Light Marrow Skin
Basic Darkest Leaf Green : White 1:1 (except Kato)
Maturing to Premo olive.

Pastels: Palest Lavender 51
Leaf Green 15
Olive 74
Dark Olive 76
Dark Leaf Colours 75 & 77

Lettuce Dark In Fimo
57 Leaf Green : Basic Summer Leaf 1:1 Hue:Trans 1:6

Lettuce Light
Basic Spring Green
Hue:Trans 1:6 - skinner shade both greens into FC2

Translucent clays

The translucent clays vary in translucency and colour. It seems strange to say that a translucent clay has a colour but remember they are not 'transparent'. That is to say they are not perfectly clear. That goal has not yet been reached because a perfectly clear filler has not yet been found to turn a liquid polymer into a solid one. Even the liquid polymer manufacturers have some problems reaching a completely clear and colourless formula. Though they are pretty close! So we have to think of them in terms of their comparative translucency. Most of them choose to have a slightly whitening filler for use as a clay on it's own. Both Premo and Kato clay however have looked for more translucency rather than a whiter colour and have a slightly pink caste which doesn't affect their ability to mix with other colours to add to the translucency. Pardo is very translucent (almost transparent) though still has a slightly white caste. Some of the translucents can have a slightly sticky feel due

In this image (below right) I've used lightest/brightest spring green with increasing proportions of translucent. I've then rolled each piece out on my pasta machine at the thinnest setting. I've used a diamond shape so you can compare the first colour with the last. You can hardly see the stages of translucency except when you see the 90% translucent up against the 0%. The colour remains similar, but it's difficult to tell how translucent it is before it's baked, because the ingredients in the clay make it look opaque until they are plasticised. For that reason you need to do your own experiments with your own brand of clay. With a denser, more opaque clay you will need a greater proportion of translucent to colour for a fruit as 'water-filled' as a grape, for example.

to minimising the fillers which makes caning a little difficult with an almost pure translucent, but this can make them a good additive to crumbly clay. I think the clay developers are still working on this and meanwhile, we all have our favourites. For adding to colour they

all serve very well as long as you don't expect a drinking glass look!

Translucency is difficult to express as print colours and sometimes when matching we go for lighter colours to express the smaller amount of overall pigment in a translucent object such as a grape. However the actual colour you need to add to translucent clay may in fact be a stronger colour than it first appears to be so you should first choose the colour and then the translucency. This might mean doing some tests before mixing a lot of clay. Also bear this in mind when using the mixes suggested by the clay companies. Often their suggestions include a percentage of white which may not be needed when mixing a more translucent colour.

For ease of talking about translucency levels in this book I often express the level in % of the whole mix

10% translucent would mean to 9 parts colour add 1 part translucent
50% translucent would mean half and half
60% translucent means 4 part colour to 6 parts translucent etc.

However to make it easier for you in the recipes I express as a ratio with the colour.

Grape Mix
Basic Spring Green - Hue:Trans 1:20

Grape Mix 2 - Basic Spring Green : Basic Summer Leaf 1:1
Hue:Trans 1:20

Grape Stalk Mix - Basic Spring Green : Basic Summer Leaf : White 1:1:1 dust with red/brown

Although I have said you must choose the colour and then the translucency you must bear in mind that the colour you use will be a strong, pure version of the colour. Not one mixed with white. There is enough of a lightening effect in the translucent to take the strength of the colour down a few points.

I don't want you to think that as you've chosen the colour first you add the translucent to the colour. You don't. Precisely the opposite, since the translucency you need is around 90-95% for grapes. If you took just 10 grams of the green mix you would need nearly a 200g of translucent to mix it to the right translucency. No, it's better to think the other way around and add your colour to the translucent. So in 10 grams of clay you would need one gram or less of colour.

The guidelines I give in this book are for information only and are from my eye for colour and translucency. But every artist is different and you shouldn't stick slavishly to my translucency any more than you should to the colour mixes.

Tip: When making grapes use the three or four at a time method shown on the cherries p27.

Dust your grapes with very fine talc before baking for the authentic 'bloom'.

Green peppers project

So, putting the translucency 'lesson' into practise:

My Italian green peppers are a 60% translucent mix. That is to say the colour is 40% of the mix or 4 parts ... (or 4 grams out of ten)
The translucent part of the mix is 60% or 6 parts or 6 grams in a small test mix
The leaves want a little less translucency, they'd be about 50%. So that would be 50% colour 50% translucent.

This is because we get the extra translucency into the leaves by making them very thin indeed!

Using your extruder

The basic spring green mix mixed down with translucent at a ratio of 4:6 makes a really nice bright vibrant mix for the Italian green peppers as they are just popping out in the garden. As they mature they get darker and so, to make a 3 mix set (that is a set of three slightly different mixes, as I did with the grapes) you should add a scrap of navy blue, mix, put some to one side and then add just a scrap more. Alternatively if you have already made up a basic summer green colour, add bits of that to 'mature' the colour a bit. This colour does suffer quite badly from the metameric effect so you may need to tweak the blue a bit for different light conditions. *See metamerism p56.*

Some of the extruders available come with a 'core extruder', I love the effect of actually making a hollow object in real life hollow in miniature. It sounds crazy to do it for a fruit (yes peppers are a fruit) that you aren't going to cut open, (although you can), but it still does look better when you do. There's a lightness both physically and visually when you do make them hollow. Extrude a piece of each of your mixes.

The little pepper shapes are closed at the top and bottom. Then with a craft tool I press gently into the sides to produce a nice indentation on 3 sides and finally just push each little pepper from each end a bit to cause it to twist or scrunch just a little as they do on the plant. In the northern European supermarkets these Italian peppers are always the biggest and the straightest available. However in a local farmers market or in

Professional tips
Play around with merging your colours using the dark on one side of a cylinder, the light on the other side and the mid colour between the two. This, where you're lucky, makes a really nice blend that looks even more realistic. Try also the 'disc extrusion technique' (look on the internet) with this. The results are some subtle and interesting blends.

the garden they can be all sorts of shapes and sizes.

The leaves are an elongated tear-drop shape and very delicate. So make the thinnest 2 colour sheet that you can. Then stretch it even more by smoothing and pulling gently.

The colour is just barely one shade darker than the peppers so I make a sheet with a spring green/summer green and white mix on one side and the darker summer green (that is to say half way between summer green and darkest green on the other. The colour doesn't change much from the top to the bottom of the plant so in this project I just make one colour of leaf.

The veins on the leaves are asymmetrical but regular so you need to consider this if using a veiner. Vein as many leaves as you can be bothered to do, and put to one side.

Stems for plants like peppers, aubergines and tomatoes are simple to make with a little fine flower wire you need a green coated wire of a mid green if you can get it although darker green is more common. Cut each wire into 3 pieces and attach three leaves to the end of each piece of stem with some 'goo'. And bake.
See p64 for goo recipe.

Bunch together the pieces, but irregularly. Fold in half and start to twist

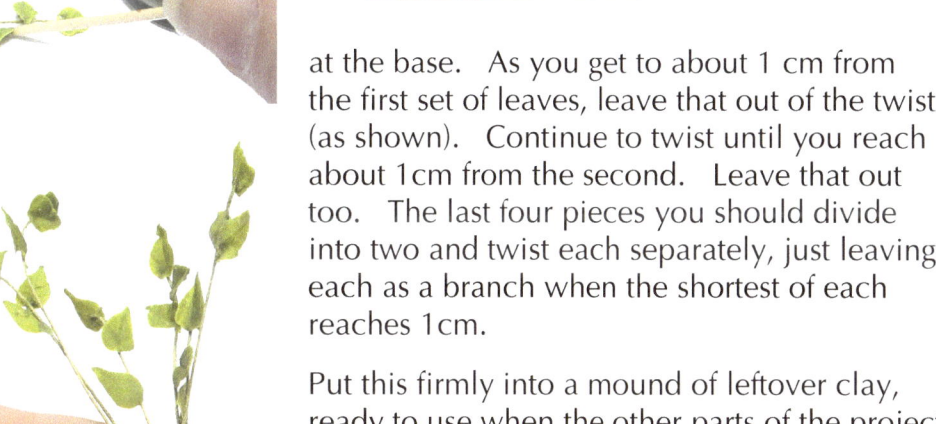

at the base. As you get to about 1 cm from the first set of leaves, leave that out of the twist (as shown). Continue to twist until you reach about 1cm from the second. Leave that out too. The last four pieces you should divide into two and twist each separately, just leaving each as a branch when the shortest of each reaches 1cm.

Put this firmly into a mound of leftover clay, ready to use when the other parts of the project are ready.

Make some little white flowers by the cut and cross method on p43. Make each of their stems curl over and bake them

You can then attach the peppers and the flowers to parts of the stem using more of the 'goo', add extra leaves where possible and re-bake the entire plant.

Bean Plant project.

Tools and materials
You really need a pasta machine for this one to get the leaves thin enough
Tiny teardrop shape cutter
Tiny printer-veiner with asymetric veins or bought tiny leaf veiner
Ball tool and Pergamano foam board or a piece of 'funky foam' (Goma eva)
Polymer clay extruder with very small hole/s
Needle ended tool, or thick upholstery pin
Cocktail stick for applying 'goo'
Softened and flexible light green clay a mixture of spring green and leftovers will do fine @ 60% translucent
Basic summer leaf green clay @ 30% translucent
Dark leaf green clay @50% translucent
Pale translucent cream clay (foundation mix see page 50)
pale yellow clay
Green 'goo' (see below)

How to make polymer clay 'goo' in medium green.
My polymer clay 'goo' is made by adding liquid polymer drop by drop to the clay until it's just runny enough to pick up with a cocktail stick without the semi solid dripping off. It needs to be really thick for a very good 'grab' like the thickest tacky glue. If you make it too thin you'll have trouble thickening it again so take it really easy.

I now use a butter knife for this job which I only use for polymer clay but you can use the back of a very strong spoon.   Chop up or grate the clay first and don't try to add too much liquid polymer at one time.   Store in a tiny jar (the individual portion jam jars are best).

See my video on **angiescarr.com/Goo**

Making the leaves
Note, after each stage cover your parts with cling film, label the parts and leave to cool.

Leaf mix.
Make a Skinner shade of the 3 greens.   Cut this sheet in half so you have 2 pieces which look the same.   Make a sandwich, offsetting

so that the mid green ends up under the dark green and fold the top over the top and the light green over the bottom.

Roll to absolutely the finest setting you can get on your machine, and then smooth out between your fingers to stretch even further until it's as thin as you can get the clay without tearing. Lay on a ceramic tile, cover in cling film and leave to cool.   Do not flatten on to the tile as it will stick and may be difficult to work with later.

The reason for making this 2 sided leaf sheet is so that the underside of each leaf can be lighter than the top and in order to make sure that all your leaves are not the same colour but a nice variety of related greens.

Stalks.

Soften your spring green clay really well, adding a touch of softener if necessary. I recommend adding a little Sculpey mould maker or you can use some flexible clay. Using an extruder with a fine holed disc, extrude a quantity of stalk material and cover and leave to cool a little.

Bean cane

You don't need much! Make a small but thick piece of summer leaf clay just mixed down with 10% pale translucent cream clay mix to lighten a bit. Roll this to your thickest setting if using a pasta machine, then on the outsides you need summer leaf mixed with 10% dark leaf clay rolled to the thinnest setting. The reason for putting this darker green layer on is when it's cut it forms a slightly darker green edge as you will see later. Roll the sandwich to the thickest setting again and cut into strips of half a centimetre wide. Cover and leave to cool ... have a cup of tea!

Flower cane

Make a very small and simple sandwich of mid green in the middle with basic pale cream on one side and basic pale cream tinted with a little golden yellow on the other side. This is because bean flowers often come in pairs, one yellow and one white. This should be rolled out on the thickest of your pasta machine settings. Put to one side. After the parts have cooled a little they should all be handleable without being too sticky.

Making Leaves

Using the Kemper tiny teardrop cutter, cut out a few dozen leaf shapes. You can change the sizes of some by gently rolling a ball tool over them on a dense sponge pad. Gently press veins into as many leaves as you can manage before you lose patience then go on to making the beans. Leaving the leaves to cool a little after handling makes them easier to assemble without 'squishing'.

Making Beans

Slice really tiny slices of your strip of bean cane and shape them on your finger so the edges are a bit thinner, you should notice that the very slightly darker edge is very realistic. The imprint your fingerprint leaves is surprisingly string-bean like! Then nip the ends into the shapes of the bottom and top of a long bean.

Very tiny flower residue can be added to this part if you're feeling really creative. You can use the pale translucent cream mix and just shave tiny bits off a little like the flower project on p43. You can 'twizzle' the top of the bean leaving a little extra at the top end to allow you to join them later. Once again when you're bored with this job ... go on to the next.

Making Flowers

Cut the flower cane in a similar way to the way you cut the bean cane to make a tiny box shape. Roll this gently into a rounded off cylinder and thin the middle with your needle ended tool or a cocktail stick.

Assembly

Add these flowers to the stems around one inch apart using the tip of a pin's worth of 'goo' - no more or they will slide about. Press very lightly so they look like a chicken coop ladder and put a little 'nick' into each 'flower' about

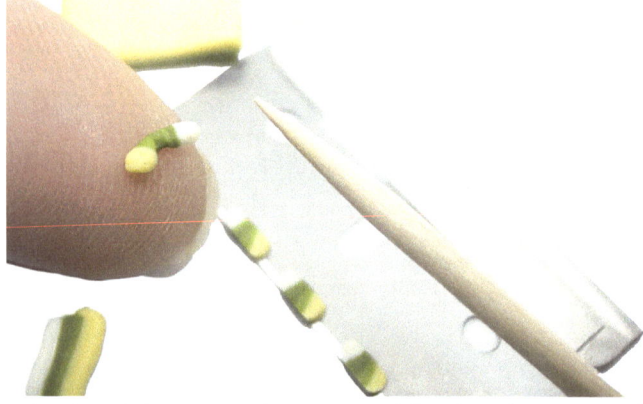

2/3rds of the way down. Add a few beans and a side stem to each of these joins, either under or over the flower. A combination is best.

To each added stem add three leaves arranged as in the photo, using a touch of 'goo' and a little pressure.

Note. *Don't worry if parts break or come apart you can either re-do them or leave them to bake separately and glue on later.*

When your stem gets to 6-8" (15-20cm) high you need to top it off with some smaller leaves. I simply subdivide the tiny leaves to nearly the base and then 'twizzle' them together to form tiny bundles of leaves. I would use the very thinnest of the clay for these leaves. Put one or two of these bundles on the top end of your stem.

Don't bake them flat!

Now carefully move from the work surface and bake on an uneven surface

Make a paper support by zigzag folding some paper. Pick up your stems very gently using your blade, and lay the stems across and/or up the paper support. This gives a nice uneven twisty look. Bake!

You can mount your beans two or three to a stake. You can also put three stakes together to form a bean pyramid. I mounted my first ones in a box made from polymer clay wood filled with polymer clay mud (coated in soil substitute) and just used my craft drill to drill holes for the ends of the bean plants and for pieces of stick which came from a bamboo place mat. Long bamboo skewers will do just as well.

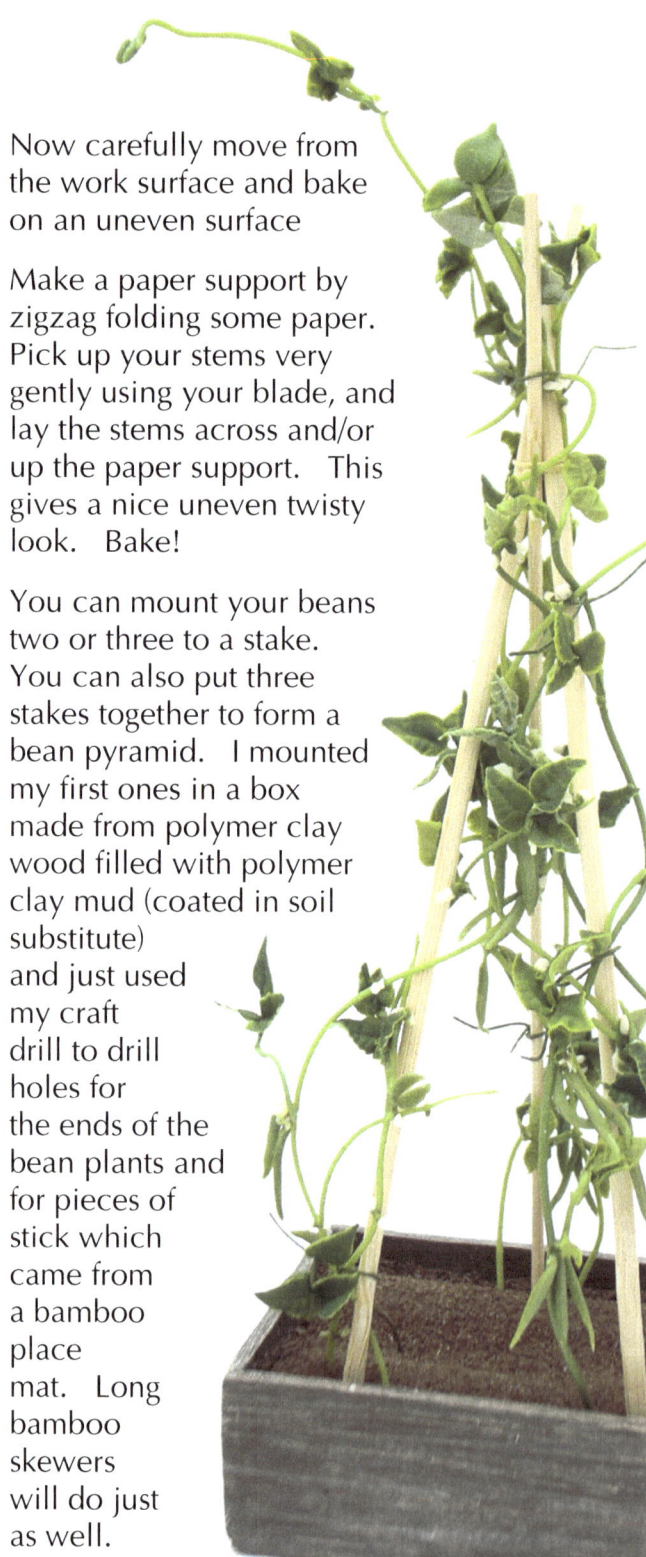

- Artichoke In Premo Olive : White
  2:1

- Asparagus In Premo
  Basic Spring Green : White
  2:1

- Brassica Leaf In Premo
  Jungle : Olive
  1:1

- Artichoke Cooked Premo
  Marine Blue : Cadmium Yellow 2:10 (inner is lighter)

- Asparagus Cooked Premo
  Zinc Yellow : Ultramarine
  10:1 Hue:Trans 4:6

- Brassica Leaf Cooked Premo
  Zinc Yellow : Ultramarine
  10:2 Hue:Trans 7:3

Raw, Cooked & Overcooked

One more thing before we leave fresh garden greens behind and delve into more unusual colours.

We're not talking about polymer clay being overcooked here. But since many people choose to make cooked food in miniature, rather than just the ingredients (which is my passion), you have to consider that the colour changes when cooking food.

Raw food especially vegetables are thoroughly covered in this book.   But what about the colours for cooked vegetables?

Firstly translucency is an issue. As, for example, a piece of asparagus is cooked it becomes slightly more translucent. I always try to get thoroughly involved with my subject. Which would naturally include cooking as well as looking. And then, naturally, eating!

On the other hand, fish *(see mackerel on p75)* will actually whiten and become more opaque in the cooking process. Cooked meats of course turn from translucent pink and red to opaque shades of brown.

Look at the green vegetables in the photograph. They are lightly cooked and so those things that looked green actually look even sharper. A little more blue in the case of the stalks and heads. The broccoli leaves, which in the garden would have a bluish powdery coating are actually a deeper fresher more saturated green and less bluish. But overcooked greens can lose almost all their blue.

So, you do need to adjust your colour mixes when making plated or cooking food from those you use for fresh garden or market produce.

CHAPTER SIX
Blue And Unusual

1	2	3
4	5	6
7	8	9

Recipe Key: 1 Premo Turquoise   2 Premo Rhino   3 p70 (Sky Blue)
 4 Cernit Blue 200   5 p53 (Mid Blue)   6 p70 (Forget Me Not)
 7 Brown & Black   8 p53 (Deep Orange)   9 p58 (Green Bean)

Photo of Møns Klint by Keld Hansen.

Blue Is Rare In Nature

It often seems as if blue is rare in living nature as it is a colour that is associated with alkaline conditions. But where blue does occur it can often be vivid and surprising. There are blue hydrangeas, morning glory iris, forget me not and of course all the bluey green tints of garden leaves such as asparagus leaves, some brassicas, lavenders, some cactuses and grasses as well as moulds and lichens. There is of course also the bright blue sky and the deep blue sea. Blue reflected in bubbles, the intense blue of a blue eye, and many other wonders of nature such as the peacock, along with other displaying birds, displays green and intense blue. Blue butterflies and blue bugs and beetles also populate our planet. Some of them cheeky enough to look metallic blue. It's a much bigger list but just a few of these colours I'll look at here.

Here are recipes for some of the blues in nature.

> Succulent / Cactus Leaves
> Jungle : Olive : White 1:1:1

> Night Sky In Cernit
> Use Navy

> Sky Blue In Premo
> White : Turquoise : Ultramarine 10:4:1

> Forget Me Not In Premo
> White : Ultramarine : Turquoise 10:2:1

Peacock Feather Cane – A Lesson In What Not To Do!

This was ultimately an unsuccessful cane because I didn't get the colour values right. That is to say I allowed all the outer parts of the feather to blend into a muddy cane and didn't follow my own guidelines on exaggeration. The idea had been to blend through from the colours of the 'eye' of the cane on one end to the colours on the other end by using opposing Skinner blends throughout the roll. I wanted to get a slight change from slice to slice. Sounds clever and looks clever in these pictures. And in fact this idea worked for the stars in a 50 Euro note that I made. However I forgot a couple of crucial things.

One was that all the colour values were going to be pretty equal, especially in the middle of the cane.

The other was that the outside feathery bits were going to turn muddy and indistinguishable. And the third problem was just how much translucent I was going to need to support it all. I ran out of the right translucent in the right clay half way through and ended blending the 'pinky' translucent with another brand. None of this worked well so that, although the unbaked cane itself looked impressive, the final result was dull. This shows that I still have a great deal to learn!

These pictures are the colours I used for the centre of the cane, from the two ends of the same mix and these are how it looked (unbaked) within the centre part of the feather.

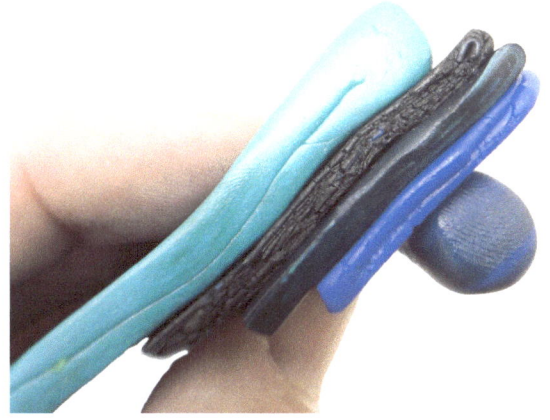
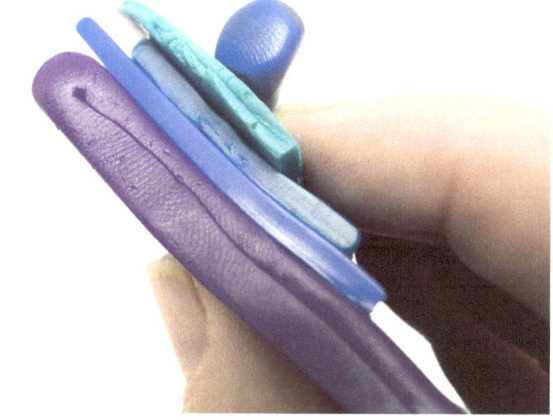

Unfortunately, some of nature's metallic colours can't be replicated in miniature in polymer clay except with the use of metallic powders. Pearlised powders can be used to 'save' a cane like this one.   And cutting very fine and laying in a fan shape on a glass pane also shows the direction I wanted to go.   But the fact remains this cane didn't 'cut it'.

Read the wonderful book Polymer Clay Colour Inspirations, by Lindley Haunani & Maggie Maggio for more information on solving this problem.

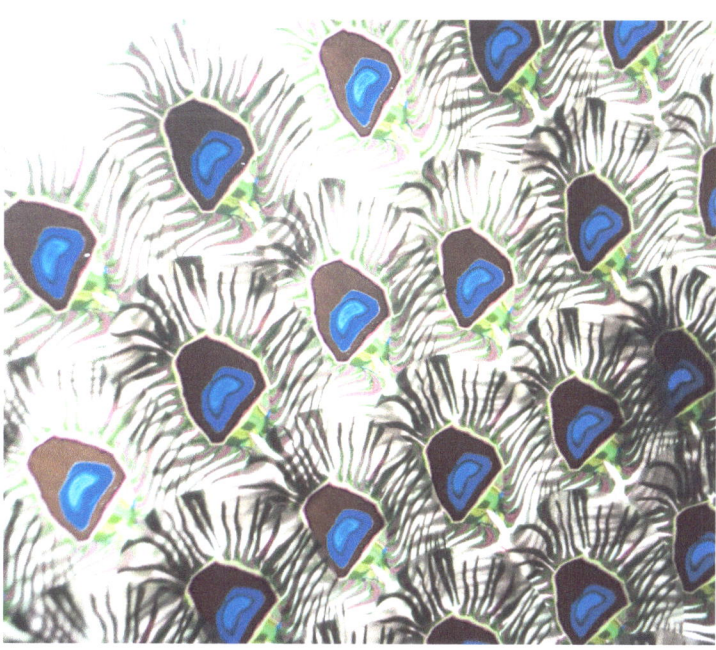

Møns Klint – Chalk-Cliffed National Park In Denmark

Here I used a Skinner shade of 3 stages. White to light turquoise, light turquoise to dark turquoise and dark turquoise to marine blue in Premo then combining into one sheet to reproduce the absolutely stunning seascape background of this beauty spot in Denmark. I am not an experienced painter, hardly having painted at all since my 20s, but the scene moved me so much I wanted to try it in polymer clay. I worked from a photograph a friend took for me at my direction when visiting the site. This meant I knew what it was I was looking for and was amazed by in the scene. I don't believe it's easy to get any life or depth into a piece of work which is only worked from photographs whether it be tiny mini vegetables, or a 'painting' without the first hand experience of the scene.

This composition I treated just as I would have a miniature . So I simplified and exaggerated to get the essence of the scene. What struck me at the site was the movement, almost a circular movement down the deep ravine to a stunning lime washed turquoise blue sea, and how the trees, though stark and closing round the pathway, didn't have an oppressive feeling but rather a 'drawing in'. And how the spring light that broke through, picked out the the copper leaves that still remained from the autumn leaf fall. I found that using a combination of really fresh blues and mica clays both in the background and the leaves in the foreground, combined with left overs mixed into several shades of brown and greenish brown low-lighted with a very dark almost black brown, gave me the essence of the scene. I used the depth of strips of clay built up over the flatness of a Skinner shaded background and added a twiggy lightness with fawn extruded clay and just a few tiny spring green touches on a very small part of the trees on the right hand side. The leaves were just flakes of copper and gold mica clay added with a hockey stick tool, on a background of chopped up brown leftovers.

Photograph of Møns Klint (left) and polymer clay (right)

The "Ugly Bug's Ball"

I found a little bug in my garden while examining colours closely. As a matter of fact my garden is full of interesting little bugs but this one struck me because it was totally metallic! Looking on the internet for "metallic bugs" I came upon the world of jewel bugs. Very aptly named critters and you can just see them at a costume ball, showing off like mannequins at the Carnivale in Venice!

I have had to abandon my miniaturist 'hat' for a day or two to play with pearlised polymer clay and metallic powders and paints to show that nature isn't devoid of jewel colours. I could of course have as easily used fish. Since the real thing is between a half and 1 centimetre, (about a quarter to less than half an inch) these bugs are just under x2 scale.

Although I really enjoyed using Premo for this project I did find that for very small bugs there is little to be gained by using pearlised clay as there is not enough visible mica to make the metallic look in something so small, and caned. I did use some in these bugs but had to augment every one with pearlised powders (pearl-ex). I didn't have any of the blue colours at the time but a turquoise colour would go nicely on with these beetles. For one-offs where the mica clays are smoothed, I think they would be more useful. Also for items like this in a larger scale pearlised powders will add brilliance.

Having made the mistake of not having enough contrast in the peacock cane I was not going to fall into that trap again! I used Premo's Peacock Blue shaded to yellow which produced a vivid green in the middle of the cane and then cut it into sections to make up all the bluey green parts.

Then I used Lindly Haunani's suggestion of using fluorescent clay to lift the red in the multicoloured stink bug. This is an interesting idea which I'm going to explore further as sometimes miniaturisation does mean that subtle colours can get lost. This little guy didn't call for any subtlety! I also outlined all the major elements in a thin layer of black. As I lengthened the cane I cut into smaller pieces and the allowed the end of the cane to 'round off', before cutting the beetle off as a fat slice and rounding and adding a few

Polymer clay bug cane in the stages of being made

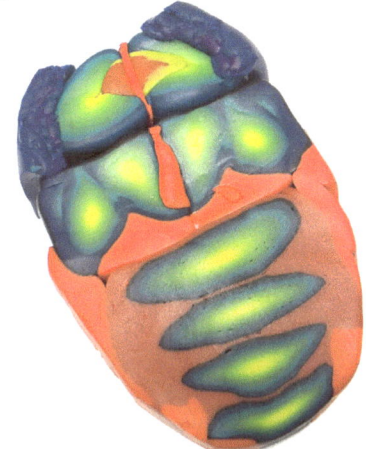

Polymer clay bug cane in the stages of being made

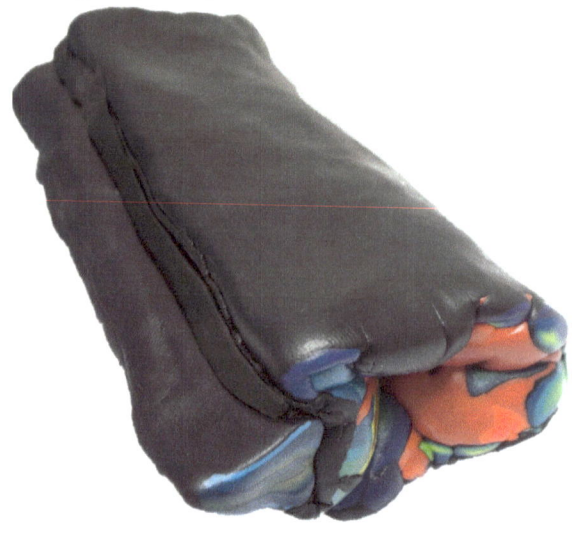

indentations to accentuate his shape. The antennae are made from wire pulled out of a metal mesh fabric and painted in Lumiere pearlised paints. The legs are just jewellery wire bent into shape and attached by more polymer clay, polymer clay 'goo' *(see p64)* and a second baking.

Knowing the rules & breaking them

Okay, I've said in nature green is not just green. And you can't just take green clay out of the packet and expect a realistic result even if your mastery of form and scale are second to none.

Yes and I've also said that not only is the authenticity of colour important but also when representing nature the relative translucency of a colour is also vital to give life to an item. For example, a grape without enough translucency might look like a pea. A lettuce might look more like a spring cabbage.

I've also voiced my opinion that when recreating nature in a smaller scale in whether in 2 or 3 dimensions the smaller the scale the more important it is to get the colour as accurate as possible because the smaller an item becomes the more it can just look like a 'blob'. If it's the wrong colour even if the form is perfect, it just won't look right, whereas if the colour is perfect even without glasses or magnifiers the audience can tell, or at least has a better chance of recognising what your work represents.

Having banged on about all that now I want to have you look at it all another way!

How about breaking some of the rules?

When you play with the colour you are playing with the mind of the viewer. In some cases this is deliberate and beautiful. For example in primitive art the colours are all strong primaries. This gives them an air of vibrancy, youth, a party atmosphere. If you do make your miniatures with the packet oranges and bright greens you can create a 'Mexican primitive' palette. Faded out colours give the impression of age ... with happy melancholy or memory. Darker dirtier neutrals especially over-opaque colours give age with heaviness, even depression. Translucency gives a 'lighter' (not heavy) look. Deliberate over-use of translucency gives an ethereal or dreamlike quality ... great in 'fairy glades' for example or to capture fleeting memories or wishful thinking!

Using the wrong colours altogether is surreal or even nightmarish.

Making A Mackerel Cane

Level – advanced to professional

You really need a bit of experience in Skinner-blending to tackle this. (A simpler blend for fish is shown in my book Making Miniature Food)

You will need:
*Fimo colours white, Translucent, Black, Metallic blue effects and metallic green effects
A scrap of golden yellow clay
A pasta machine
A 'wavy' blade
A single sided blade
A very fine holed piping nozzle.
Liquid Fimo (for 'glueing')*

The essence of this cane is to get a gentle blend between black, navy blue, greenish blue and white.

This means cutting up a complicated Skinner blend into 4 easier parts. We want a blend from black to metallic blue, one from metallic blue to green, one from green to white(ish) and the last one from your first white which might have picked up a little blue and green to a 'clean' white

I use Fimo for this job because of it's usability when caning and because it has the metallic blue and green that I want in the 'Effects' range. Translucent is now also in the 'Effects' range and is called translucent white.

You mix and prepare each of your colours in this order because happiness is a clean pasta machine! So even though it seems counter-intuitive I start off with black this time, and move through the colours to white. The first white makes the blend gentler and cleans your pasta machine at the same time! Whatever size your mix is you need to make extra white for the fish 'belly'. N.B. I add translucent to each and every one of these colours to give them all a slight translucency and also to make the clay softer and easier to blend together.

First prepare a square of black, two of blue, two of green and three of white. Then cut your squares diagonally and stack one half

on the other to form the triangles shown. Technically, if you use a small enough amount of clay, you could then push all these squares together and blend as one strip. But because of the way we then want to change direction to stack the blend I prefer to make the blend in separate sections.

If you have never made a Skinner blend before please refer to one of my books or any good polymer clay tutorial book or on the internet. Basically however, the technique is to pass the square through the machine in one direction and then fold up the clay in the same direction and pass through again, repeating this step until the clay is thoroughly and smoothly blended. The important thing is to remember never to reverse the direction until the clay is fully blended.

You should end up with 4 smooth blends. Then you take each piece and pass it through the machine in the opposite direction. That is to say from the darker to the lighter colour. I pass it through twice.

Once on the same setting. Then I take the setting down one (or two depending on your pasta machine) to form a longer strip shaded from one end to the other.

Then stack up the colours by folding the clay over and over, pressing gently and smoothing out any air from between the sheets.

Cut off a piece between 1/4 and 1/3 of the entire stack. Put this aside to use later for the 'head' cane.

Take a wavy blade and cut right through the cane several times. Make a thick sheet of black clay and tear the edge (to make sure it's irregular) and insert the clay up to, but not beyond, the place where the colour changes to white.

Add black spots by inserting a thick knitting needle in a few places and feeding a 'bootlace' sized roll of black clay into each.

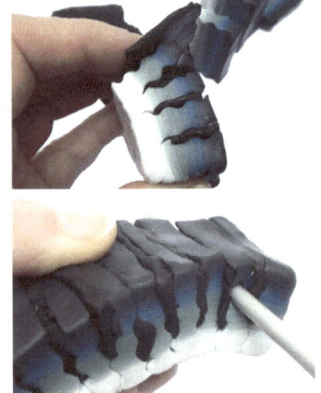

Press everything back into shape to form an elongated curvy triangle fish body shape. Add extra white to form a 'belly that is about 50% of the whole shape.

Lengthen this cane part way so that you can cut a piece solely to use for skin on fillets.

The other piece will have a head cane inserted into it.

Fish head cane

First form an eye cane with a black cane surrounded by the eye colour. I've used yellow for the eye because a mackerel eye is yellowish. The colour should be bright and opaque rather than translucent, because the eye is so small it will hardly be seen otherwise, so the contrast must be strong. Then surround with a sheet of black again just to highlight the edge.

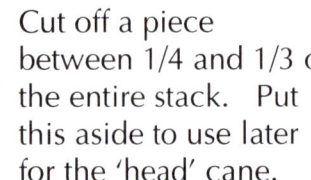

Insert the eye cane into the middle of the extra piece of cane which you had put to one side. You can either part the colours again or cut into them. I recommend you make a circular indentation with a knitting needle or a pencil to 'let' the eye into. Just to avoid squashing the eye shape when putting back together.

Adding the head to the body cane

Cut a small v shape into the body cane and form the head cane into a diamond shape to fit into it. Insert the head cane into this triangle and curve the body round the head.

This cane is now ready to lengthen to your desired scale.

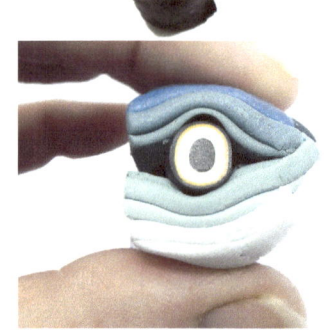

I recommend you keep some only part lengthened because it's easier to re-condition a larger cane while lengthening it if it gets a bit old or cold. Just take a small piece right down to the scale you're using. (12th scale approx. shown).

Cut thick slices (approximately 3-4mm) off your cane and shape the fish on your index finger to curve off the sharp edges. I recommend you look at pictures of mackerel on the internet to get the shape right.

You can add the tail one of two ways. The easiest way is to lift the end of the body and put the tail ... with a dab of Liquid Fimo on it, under the end of the body. Or if you're making a fish which will be seen from both sides you need carefully to make a little slit in the body and insert a piece of tail into the slit. Any badly cut shavings from the tail cane can be used to cut tiny slivers for the side fin. Mark a downward turning mouth, I use my fingernail for this, a couple of curved lines for the gills and if you like you can accentuate the eyes using a tiny piping nozzle.

I use sugarcraft powders to add a little fishy sheen and finish off with a semi-matte varnish. I recommend the Cernit solvent based varnish for this. Their matte varnish has a very slight sheen which I like but if you want a wetter look use the gloss one.

Making tail and fins

Make a stack of left over colours and translucent. The mix and pattern for this can depend on what clay you have left over but should contain some black and some translucent lines. Cut and stack several times until the lines are fine but visible (5 or 6 times). You should attempt to make your stack long and thin as in the picture.

Cut out a triangle, squeeze down one side of this cane to form a tail fin shape and lengthen. Bake this tail cane as it is easier to cut very fine when pre baked. Practise cutting the tail fin very fine with a single sided blade. I never use a surgical blade for this job because the baked clay is quite hard and may shatter the blade.

Making a fish fillet

Cut thin slices of the fish cane without the head or tail and press these on a thin sheet of clay in the right colour for your fish. I use Cernit's doll colours for this job because of the relative translucency. The colour 'Biscuit' in the Cernit range is perfect for raw mackerel fillets. For cooked add just a little white (any type of white clay will do).

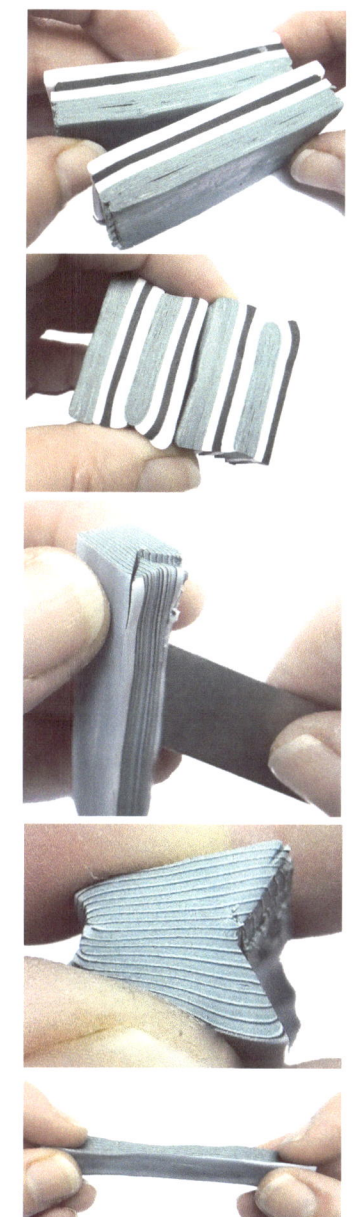

CHAPTER SEVEN
Brown

1	2	3
4	5	6
7	8	9

Recipe Key: 1 p52 (Walnut)   2 p51 (Burnt Umber)   3 p51 (Terracotta)

4 Ochre   5 p51 (Ecru)   6 Umber & Grey

7 p53 (Light Caramel)   8 p53 (Chocolate Milk)   9 p51 (Sienna)

Boletus-Style Mushroom (Easy)

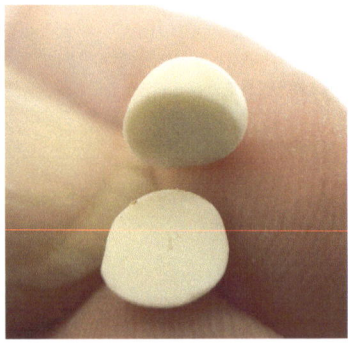
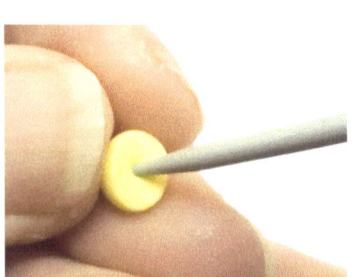
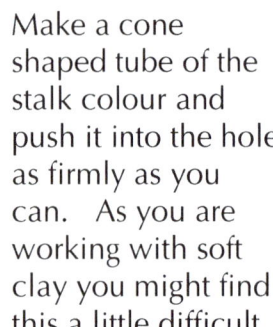
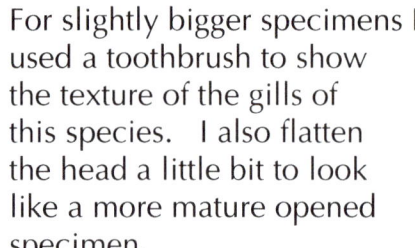

Roll a tiny ball of clay of the main colour of the mushroom 'gills' and cut it in half.

Using a small knitting needle push a hole deeply in the underside of the half.

Make a cone shaped tube of the stalk colour and push it into the hole as firmly as you can. As you are working with soft clay you might find this a little difficult to do without distorting one or other part but if you practise on this one you'll find the other mushrooms easier to make. It can help to push the needle right through the cap until it shows on the surface and then push the stalk through and smooth it off at the top. This really bonds the two parts together. I've tried making the stalk separately but this way really bonds better.

Cut the stalk off and form the end into a nice bulbous shape. Wild mushrooms are usually pulled rather than cut.

For slightly bigger specimens I used a toothbrush to show the texture of the gills of this species. I also flatten the head a little bit to look like a more mature opened specimen.

If the surface of your mushroom has a different colour, as it is in the case of this boletus, my first method is to colour it with powder or decorating chalk. A good place to source decorating powders is cake craft shops but other sources are craft shops and you can also use scraped off pastel chalks or even make-up colours.

Almost wherever you're living there will be regional wild mushrooms. Even in the heart of the city there will be wholefood or specialist delicatessen shops who will

stock wild mushrooms in season. However. If you're making the miniature version out of season then the internet will help with photographs as well as information on type, form colour and habitat. For example try going to Google Images. A wealth of beautiful images will appear.

Note, if you're working from photographs, make sure you work from several as image quality and print colours can vary.

A bit of research into seasonality and regionality.

When deciding on miniature foods, flowers and natures bounty to make for your garden or even for the shops, think about the season.

If you are working from life, or pinning down colours and descriptions for later you will already know the season. But if working from photos do your homework. This applies to colours especially!

Often when collecting or making miniature foods we do forget regional variety and season. It's OK in a modern dollshouse to put vegetables together that grow at different seasons for example. Because modern supermarkets do have imported goods. But don't put one seasons fruit and vegetables with those that mature at a different time of year in a 1950s or earlier dollshouse. The very rich may have been able to import the odd exotic item but any normal household would never get strawberries and winter brassicas or leeks together. And remember the seasons for wild mushrooms!

I bake all my mushrooms before gluing into the basket and of course, when making deep baskets I 'cheat' a little at the bottom. There are some mushrooms called Amanita Ponderosa (very popular and known as 'gurumelos' in Andalucia). When they are young they are just like a blob with a conical base called a volva, and they are usually just a dirtied white. They are so easy to make I just put lots in the bottom of baskets to save work! The dirt depends upon where you find your mushrooms. In this case it's a deep golden brown sandy soil. But even mud is not just mud! And some mushrooms grow in leaf mould. Don't forget your research here either.

real 'gurumelos' freshly picked

Autumn leaves

Depending on the area of the world and the country, the speed of change of weather and even acidity etc. of the soil autumn leaves can

be dull browns or spectacular golden, ochre, orange, red even purple!   So even browns can be colourful.

A little metallic clay can help give them extra luminescence.   I add copper to reddish leaves and gold to golden leaves.   I like the Premo colours for this as their mica seems to be very fine and produce a more beautiful mica-shift effect without necessarily looking so 'glittery'. Making the clay into a Skinner shaded roll helps give a 3 dimensional effect to the leaves.   Here I've used a mix of terracotta with copper mica clay and ochre mixed with gold mica clay.   All 5 of the leaves are made with the same cane.   Once again I've used that little 'cheat' as I do with the poinsettias on p31 to make

a stronger definition in the veins . I've tried doing it without but brown is a very muddy colour and can suffer even worse from loss of definition so I use spring green bordered by a very dark (nearly black) green.   The very edges of the leaves also have a very fine border (skin) on the cane.   Fineness to this skin was achieved by making all the leaf parts as one large cane and then dividing it into 5.   I used the slightly 'dodgy' ends to make the smallest leaves because the way the clay had folded in on itself made it look like a curled leaf. Another case where chance can augment art! Because this leaf is complicated and also has a 'toothed' edge I used a translucent support between the leaves which I used to take the cane to a certain scale and then cut out most of the translucent just leaving the support in the 'teeth'.   And then I lengthened it a little more.

I also use Cernit glamour copper (mica clay) when making chestnuts. *See p12.* I chose this clay for chestnuts as it has a very subtle natural sheen when baked.   Once again I exaggerated the lines a bit with darker brown and black. The end colour of the chestnuts are made by leaving the inside of the cane showing at the ends.

Saving leftover clays

I use a lot if clay, so it's definitely worth my while saving leftover clays and putting them to good use. My first and favourite option is to re-combine leftovers back into the next production of the cane the original came from. This is where an intermediate colour is required. For example the leftovers from a strawberry cane can be re-combined back into the pink of the next strawberry cane. The leftovers from a mushroom cane forms the middle 'mushroomy' colours for my next mushroom cane. Lefty over greens from mixed cabbage colours, leeks, limes etc. go to make the mix for a new lighter colour cane.

The next stage would be to use colours which mix down to form another colour. Left overs from an orange cane and a strawberry cane are quite a good combination for tomatoes. Lemon canes can go into lighter greens in my cabbages. Pineapple colours can go into sweetcorn or butter or cheese mixes. It's not always that easy of course. When a lump of left over clay has more than one base colour you can't separate them and your only alternative is to use it for 'muddier' colours. Still, it's a very good idea to make different shades of 'mud' by separating the different types of leftovers into ones with more white, or ones with more dark colours etc. This helps you to select colours which will more easily mix down to the shade you need with the addition of other (new) colours.

Other uses for leftovers would be: light and translucent colours can go inside canes with skins on like whole apples tomatoes oranges etc. Leftover greens can form the inside of cabbages etc., greens and browns can also be mixed up, extruded and pre-baked for stalks and stems of flowers and plants.

Professional tip

This is a piece of advice I rarely follow myself, and end up kicking myself for not doing so. If you have a large quantity of leftover, from a particularly big cane, it's really worth mixing up and then taking ... and baking a sample piece which you can then attach to the plastic bag or tub you keep this clay in. This helps you gauge the level of translucency, and the baked colour of the clay, both of which could be significantly different from the appearance of the unbaked clay. It's also worth taking a note of the cane it came from, and any use you think it may be put to in future, as you can easily forget ideas among piles and piles of left over clay and end up opening new packets to be 'on the safe side'.

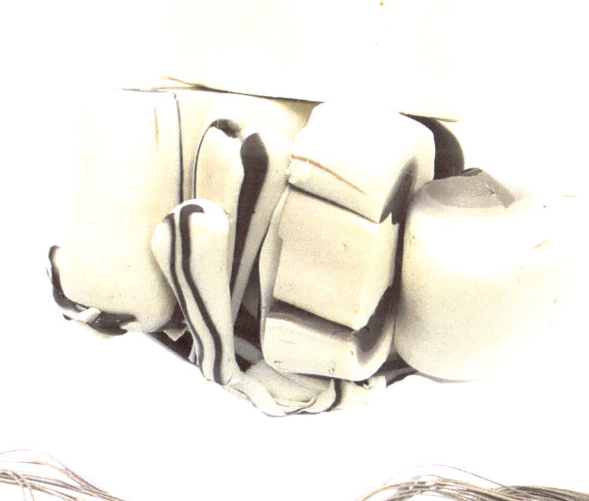

Leftover clay labelled with test squares

Brown Paper Bags

Brown paper is fairly easy to simulate in polymer clay and is cheap in materials as you can recycle all your old bits of clay into the browns you'll need.

You will need a pasta machine and plenty of old clay leftovers for this 'recycling' project! You'll also need talcum powder to keep the clay from sticking to your fingers. You need to make sure the nails of your little fingers aren't too long or you will find this project difficult to get right.

Firstly take a pile of old leftovers and mix together and condition really well. If you find your mix is a bit dull for brown paper add a bit of orange. If it's too dark add a bit of white or light grey base. Generally, If you're a regular clay user, you'll have enough leftovers of different colours to be able to make a good brown paper colour. Start with a smallish amount and add until you're happy with the result. If you don't have any brown paper in the house to check your mix against you can use the colour of light wood furniture or a sisal rug to check against as they are all similar colours. Then you need to mix a similar but slightly lighter colour. you can do this by taking just less than half of your clay and adding some white.

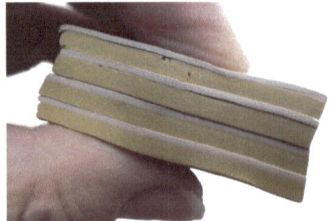

Make 2 squares, one of each colour of clay, the same size and thickness. If using a pasta machine you should set it on the thickest setting.

Stack these squares one on top of another and then cut the resultant stack in half and place one on top of the other again. Make sure that you always keep the colours alternated otherwise you'll have some thicker bands in your mix. Do this several times 4 in total.

Press your stack down until it is around 1cm in depth. You will find some of your stack 'spreads' so not all of it will be usable. It's a good idea to trim the edges back until all the lines are as tidy and straight as possible.

Slice thin slices off your stack and join

them together to form a thin sheet. This sheet should end up around 4-5 cm wide.

Press and smooth the joins to form a good bond. This is important, as if the bond is not good enough the pieces will part when you roll them thinner.

Pass this sheet through the pasta machine in the direction of the stripes to thin it out. You may need to do this twice. Once on a medium setting and once on a very thin setting.

It's worth practising making these paper bags on a fairly thin setting first and then when you get successful at it ... go thinner. Obviously the thinner you can make it ... the more realistic.

Cut the resulting sheet into sections of around 2cm long and around 4 wide and wrap one round your dry and very slightly talcum powdered finger.

Make a slight overlap and press this overlap to seal it. It's very important that you get the level of talcum powder right. You

need very little. Too much and the ends won't seal.

Slide the little cylinder you have just formed off your finger and press down the bottom edge to join it. It's best if you have a thin strip of wood or card for this. In this picture I'm using the edge of an unopened blade pack.

Once joined you can arrange your bag into a standing up or falling down position using your finger again to press the base down onto your baking surface.

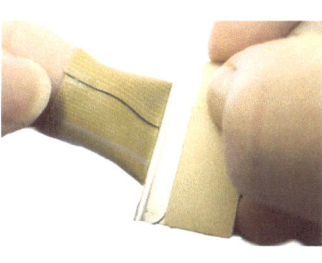

You can fill the bag at this stage if you like with semolina/lentils etc. to 'blind bake' it with a 'filled' shape. You will pre-bake your bags before filling them with fruit etc as the process of filling can tear the very thin clay.

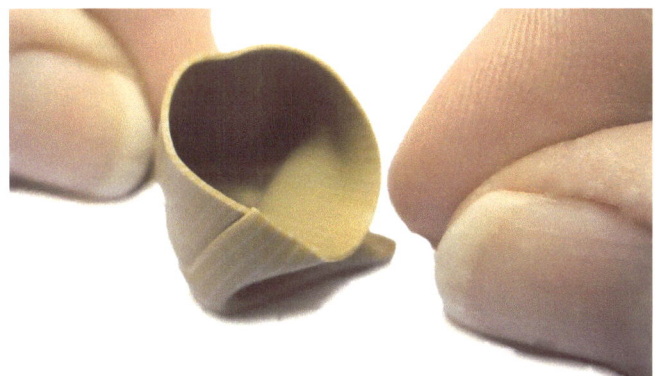

Wood!

What better use for your leftovers than to blend them up and make different shades of wood sheeting for using just like real wood. You can make fat polymer clay 'sleepers' for raised bed gardens right down to thin veneers. The main problem you will find is getting the grain fine enough while still seeing that there is a grain. There are several tutorials on the internet with many complicated steps. All in the name of getting a randomness to the lines of the grain. They are all worth following to find your favourite. I've taken a combination of several ideas and it seems to work, but lets face it the one thing you can afford to experiment with is leftovers. What can go wrong? If it doesn't work you just start again making a very slightly different shade!

My advice is not to worry about the shade or item you want to achieve first. This is playtime! Get a handful of leftovers that make a nice light brown mix, then all the other colours should total about half the quantity of the main colours. Lay a thick sheet or sheets of the lightest or the main colours of your wood on your working board.

I've used 2 main colours here. Use leftovers mixed with black for dark dull colours. Mixed with white for bright brown colours. Mixed with white and a little yellow for golden woods and with both white and black for a greyed out look. Make sure that there are both dull and brighter colours. You can even use the mica shift metallics in small amounts to add a bit of interest. I've used Premo gold in this example because Premo's mica is really fine!

Make a stack of other mixes of leftovers both light and dark. Make this stack really rough and random. Squash these other colours together fairly randomly and slice with a straight or wavy blade into irregular pieces.

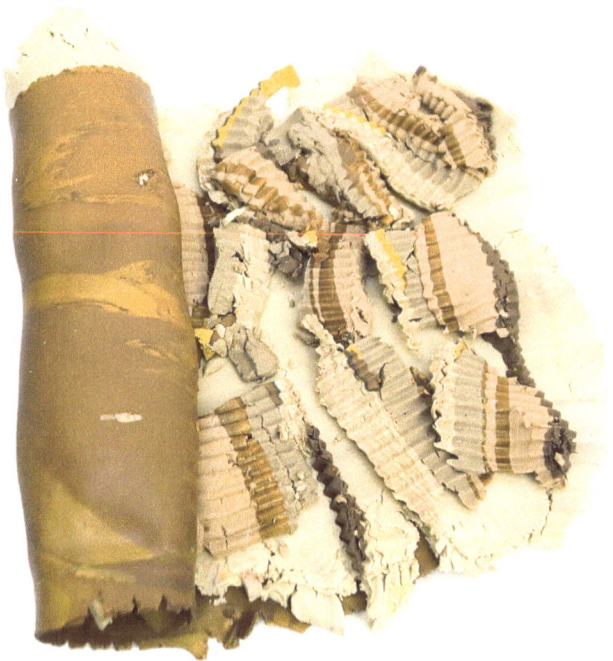

Lay these pieces across the main sheet and press down.

This is where this method overlaps with Bob Wiley's brilliant method for making wood veneer which he uses with simple layers of mica clays. Bob's method is just too subtle for anything in a smaller scale where you need a bit more exaggeration to the lines.

Take the sheet with overlays you have created and roll it up into a sausage. Take both ends of the sausage and twist twist twist. Keep on twisting until it's not only very tightly twisted but also very much narrower. Form this cylinder into a block and slice the block into long wedges. Overlap the wedges back into a sheet. Squeeze the sheet on both sides to make the grain pattern tighter until you get a

grain width that's appealing to you. If it's still too wide cut into two. Put the two widths side by side and press together again. Note:

the narrower you want your grain, the higher the contrast you'll need between colours. Depending on how you want to use the wood.

Then roll out your strip, with the grain going lengthwise, at the desired thickness. For example, for a plank use full pasta machine thickness. For a sleeper you'll need to add layers together. For a miniature chopping board the next or two sizes smaller and for thin wood and veneer you'll need to roll out on one of the thinner settings.

You do not want your 'wood' to have an over shiny finish. But you do want it to bake flat to avoid Air bubbles So I lay the slices out on a piece of rough veneer or a cheap wooden chopping board (bought for the purpose) and place another one on top. I then put this 'sandwich between two ceramic tiles to bake flat. You can then treat it like a soft and very easy to work wood strip or veneer. But of course you're going to have to sand off the shine unless you want a shiny look that is! To make trugs, crates, boxes planters etc. remember the very thin layers are flexible and may not behave in the same way as wood. But, on the plus side, you can cut with a craft knife! In this illustration, after baking I cut into pieces and reassembled into a strip of cutting boards. I filled the gaps with liquid polymer coloured and mixed with a little sanding dust from previous projects. I then baked the strip again before finally slicing to the size of boards that I needed.

CHAPTER EIGHT
Neutrals

1	2	3
4	5	6
7	8	9

All these formulas have added grey to make neutral colours. Many of the neutrals are greyed-out versions of the browns but position 5 appears on p92 as Purple For Clam Shells Pastels 67&46. Position 3 is similar to Premo Rhino and position 6 is similar to Premo Stone, these make good bases for these colours. Try adding ochres and browns and using leftovers.

Grey

One of the problems I came across again and again trying to put together the neutral recipes for this book was the different levels of saturation in the blacks put out by the different clay brands. At the same time there was a thicker and more opaque (more whitener) white in some brands than others. As a matter of fact this is true of all the colours but became especially problematical when trying out different recipes, and trying to make a formula which covered all.

I gave up temporarily on the formula because as I've said more than once, colours and formulas change and I would be giving information as fact which could shift at any time. Suffice it to say, at the time of writing this book, to get general mixing 'greys' which will (temporarily) give you a reasonably reliable result you need to use the chart below.

What I've said about checking your colours regularly goes double on these grey mixes as the brand formulae can change at any time.

To get some really subtle neutral tones try mixing colour in with a grey base. The best mix to start with is the light grey mix. But if you need a strong 'neutralised' colour use the medium one. The darker greys can be used for 'slate' colours. You will also find the greys very useful for turning your leftover clay mixes into useful brown colours especially good for aged wood or driftwood type colours and 'scrubbed' chopping boards. You will find many of the recipes in this chapter use a grey base and there are also a few grey base mixes in the main colour pages. Make up base mixes in your favourite clay so you always have some to hand. They're especially useful for seashells too. *See p92.*

Colour	Dukit	Premo	Cernit	Kato	Pardo	Fimo
Light Grey White:Black	7.5:1	6:1	22:1	4:1	25:1	25:1
Mid Grey	4:1	2:1	11:1	2:1	20:1	20:1
Dark Grey	1.5:1	1:1	4:1	5:6	9:1	8:1

Neutrals Stone marble granite and a trip to the seaside

Sometimes you have to go further afield for inspiration. This is especially true of minerals. A walk around an area will tell you what colour the local stone is. I'm lucky because I live near Riotinto where stone seems to be

every colour of the rainbow including some lovely shimmering mica colours. Neutrals don't have to be dull, and yes, stone is a natural colour and can easily be simulated in polymer clay. There are, in fact many polymer clay jewellery artists who specialise in faux mineral effects. When using their techniques remember, some of their detail may be lost when making miniatures so you may have to exaggerate the difference between colours. This means adding lightness to one colour to balance the darker clays you would use to add spots stripes or inclusions. I've included minerals in my natures colours book as I don't want to exclude inanimate natural objects from a study of nature's colours even though it's not an area of expertise for me. Besides, when recreating a scene you do need a background or a context. Stone colours are used for worktops etc in kitchens. So, when making food scenes, stone and marble colours can also be useful.

The clay manufacturers do make some nice clays with inclusions to simulate natural materials, but here again, for miniaturists the scale may be wrong. That is to say the size of particles and distance between particles may be wrong for the scale you're working to.

Dry Sage Green In Fimo
Basic Summer Leaf : Champagne : Mid Grey Base
1:4:4

Marble
Use any/all Grey Base plus FC1 or FC2
1:10 mix roughly and roll.

A trip to the seaside!   Shellfish ... Stones and Pebbles.

If you're making a scene of your own sea shore area you'll find that a trip to the seaside to collect fragments of the variety of colours from the types of rocks that you find there, along with the shells that wash up on your local beach will help you set the colour palette and you may find useful mould making materials in the smaller shells on the beach. See my book Simple Mold Making for ideas.

Here's a very simple clam shell using Dukit Pearl and Grey straight from the pack, with just a little ochre to take the brilliance off .

pebbles and are often more grey sometimes with hints of pinks and purples.   This, of course, depends on the shells available at your seaside. At Punta Umbria, an hour or so away from my home you can find the famous baby clams (coquinas) which have quite deep purple insides to their shells. On the same beach you can find very fine light weight 'mica' looking shells in yellow, pink and white.

Clays to use from the pack and intermix include Pearl clay grey and grey brown clays, ecru and champagne colour clays, ochre clay, dusting powders in browns greys greens and ochres.   Even some pinks and purples for shells.

Shells
Use Ochre, Ecru, Greys and Pale Translucent Cream

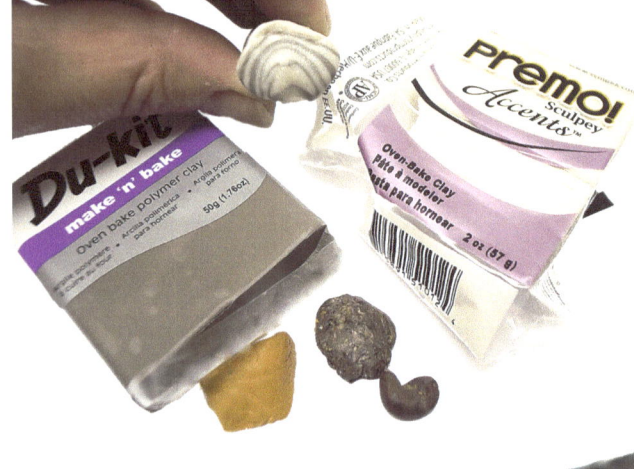

Purple for clam shells Pastels 67 & 46

real cooked baby clams (coquinas)

After making clam shells use the same colours to make some of your stones. This makes sense since shellfish do try to camouflage themselves in their habitat. I've noticed that cockle shells, where I've seen them at least, have similar colours to sand (the brown to pale ochre spectrum) but clam shells and clean oyster shells like the larger stones and

Finishes- Varnishing

Aubergines before and after subtle varnishing.

I've included varnishing because a colour can be enhanced by varnishing and also some natural forms are naturally shiny, or you may want to simulate wetness.

Some pieces of work require varnishing. However varnishing too heavily on a small piece can look ugly, out of scale and amateurish. It's worth seeing if what you really need is to sand and buff which is more time consuming of course but which can give a really beautiful finish. Many jewellery makers choose not to use varnish at all.

There is nothing worse on a miniature or a natural form than a thick 'gloopy' varnish.

My solution for this is to put the varnish on and then wipe it straight off again. You have to make sure you use something which won't leave lint or dust etc. on the item. I often use just a clean finger. Fimo have discontinued their solvent based varnish in the 'purge of all things toxic' back in the early 2000s and I've never found anything which is quite as good however I quite like the Cernit matte varnish which is actually satin.

The manufacturer recommends cleaning pieces with alcohol before varnishing to remove surface oils (some clays have an oilier surface after baking than others). Some varnishes can crackle after a certain time as they do not resist the plasticizer very well. But thinning the layer of varnish can minimise this effect too.

Good varnishes for polymer clay can be difficult to get hold of and many people are now turning to using 'wax' materials (which probably also contain silicone) rather than varnish to finish pieces of jewellery. I believe 'wax' has a similar application in miniatures to avoid the 'over-glossy' thick and detail clogging properties of varnish.

12th scale fish display

Bacalao (salt cod) more additives for surface effects

Before the advent of home freezing Cod was once preserved by heavy salting. To simulate salt micro bead and powder fillers (often sold in modelling shops as scenic snow products) make an excellent surface effect. You should be sure to pick a a nice slightly 'off' white and it's also very pleasant for handling and shaping. This is a lovely and really simple project. You'll need a tear drop shaped cutter and a heart shaped cutter. Or you can cut freehand. You also need some scenic snow and possibly some microbeads (both available from Deluxe Materials) and some black powder or chalk. You can also mix in a bit of grey and brown chalks for subtle shading.

Roll the clay out on a moderate to thick setting on your pasta machine or roll by hand using a couple of thin knitting needles as guides if this helps you. It's not vital that the sheet is perfect. Cut out a teardrop shape and from the bottom of that, cut off the very end

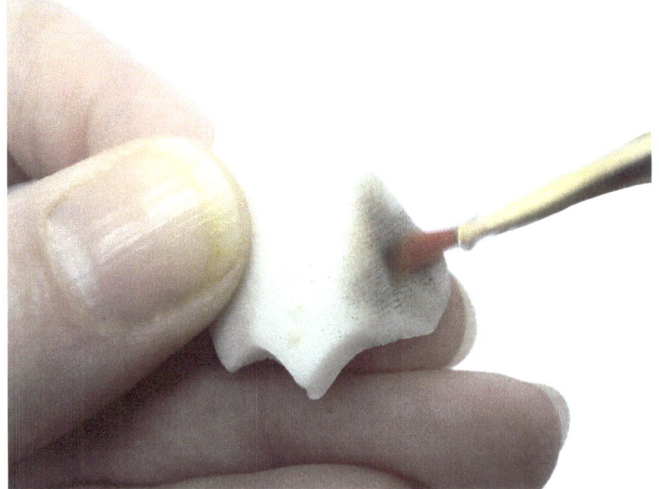

fine enough grade for the scale of your work. Since I am unable to test/verify these many materials for toxicity when heated to usual clay baking temperatures I can't recommend baking in the home oven and you should use glue or varnish to coat your work and stick the material to the clay. However I have found in my own experiments that the slight melting of this material can actually improve the adhesion and look of the finished piece. I use Cernit doll porcelain colour to make salt cod because it has a nice level of translucency,

using a fairly large heart shape cutter. This leaves you with the basic salt cod shape.

Conte carres colours for shading 42, 33, 54

Since salt cod is only available in a few places these days, and is rather expensive, you'll have to look at the picture, or a picture online to get the idea. The black bits I call 'wing' shapes are actually the belly of the fish as it's cut open and opened out leaving the back joined together and usually leaving the spine in place. The top end is where the head has been cut off prior to salting.

Press the two 'wing' shapes to flatten them. And push the centre bit inwards a bit to form a slight mound. Make some texture marks where the spine bones would be and you can add some tiny scraps of creamy clay here. You can add some subtle texture to the rest of the fish shape. Pull out, twist and flatten the tail. The tail of course can not be split in half so it simply stays where it is and looks twisted relative to the opened out fish. With a soft brush apply grey dusting to the wing shapes and the tail. If you're doing the back bear in mind that the centre is darker grey than the edge which is a more creamy colour, and you can add little grey fins to each side. I baked the salt cod at this stage, then painted with Liquid Polymer and scenic snow and baked again.

More use of pearlised and metallic powder. Fish skins.

One of the best ways to simulate the gleam of a fresh fish's skin or the glitter of another fish's scales is to use pearlised and metallic powders. Over the years I have collected a large quantity of pearly, mica and metallic powders. Even just within the white/cream range I have many different hues and particle sizes. I used a pearly powder for the scallop shells. A smooth skinned fish needs the sheen of a very fine pearlised powder such as pearl-ex which I use sparingly for my mackerel. But scales look best when made with a slightly larger particle 'glittering' powder. My favourite is a cake decorators edible lustre powder called 'Snowflake' which I've used for these sardines. For salmon I use a smooth powder on the belly and a deep silver metallic powder on the back. These differences are subtle but give the whole scene depth and variety.

There is also a cake dusting powder with an 'iris' hue. Which makes the belly of smaller fish look really gleaming, and so make the fish themselves look very fresh. You can use red or pink powders for dusting the gills and mouth pink etc. but this should be very subtle.

Bacalao In Cernit Porcelain (Doll)

But when you want to delve a little more into the gruesome reality of a fish shop you can make fish blood with a heavy dusting with one of the sanguine and adding purplish powder colours can make a realistically gruesome pile of 'entrails'.

Pastel for sardine gills "tile" 79

CHAPTER NINE
Last Word In Colour

1	2	3
4	5	6
7	8	9

Recipe Key: 1 p53 (Chocolate Milk)   2 p51 (Premo Ecru)   3 p53 (Sky Blue)

4 p48 Ruby Red   5 p53 (Rose)   6 p53 (Pale Rose)

7 p51 (Jungle)   8 p51 (Champagne)   9 p53 (Powder Puff Pink)

Opinions

During my research for this book I asked a few questions, about colour and light, of people who's opinions I value. Here are some of their most 'illuminating' (pun intended) answers which I wanted to share with you.

Talking with Tony Aquino of Van Aken (Kato clay) about pigments, and relative translucency and opacity

Tony is not a chemist but a colour formulator, with long experience in many artist media. He has been working in colouring modelling clays for around 25 years. He was very generous with his information and answered my many questions openly and thoughtfully. I was particularly pleased to hear from him because Kato clay is the one clay which I know has tackled this problem head on and produces the saturated pigments to allow the artist to be completely in control of their colour mixes.

> *"There are many extender pigments or fillers that could be added, but those additions will also add dryness and firmness and could possibly reduce pliability and sculptural properties. I am always leery of post additives to polymer clay because in many ways it does not behave like your typical art product, plus there is always a possibility of incompatibility ... [causing] polymer clays lacking consistency in viscosity from batch to batch. In all my years of working with art products, it (polymer clay) is by far the quirkiest of them all! The most effective opaque pigment would be titanium dioxide, but it also adds whiteness, so minimal amounts should be used. You can achieve the same results without the hassle of mixing in the powder, by using white clay. All other pigments, in my opinion, would require more amounts but could create the chemical change of properties that I mentioned before. So, I do not endorse post additions of extender pigments to polymer clay. Kato concentrates could provide a solution to [the problem of] increasing opacity and color strength at the same time."*

I asked Carmen Naran, who is a talented Spanish miniaturist with her own beautiful style, what type of light she works in, what is her favourite material and what colour mixing problems she encounters. She said that she both works in and photographs in the natural daylight of her own patio to avoid any shadows which might change the real colours. She always uses Fimo and adds final touches of colour with pastel chalks. She takes a lot of trouble putting just the right amount and colour of pastel on her work so as not to affect the level of translucency and so she saves an example of each of her pastel finishes to remember them for later.

Then I asked up and coming young miniaturist Myoung Jang from Korea who's use of colour and translucency are startlingly realistic what materials she uses and I was very surprised to hear that she works in Modena air drying polymer clay and her work is not caned, nor is the clay coloured although it looks like it must be. She uses acrylic paint and varnish to colour the surface. This goes full circle and

shows that it is possible to achieve stunning effects of lightness and realism in solid modelling clay and paint. Myoung also works in natural daylight, but often photographs in artificial light. These tomatoes however are photographed in the same daylight that she works in.

And finally I spoke to Linda Cummings who works in the North of England where the light levels can sometimes be quite low, and the days short in winter, about how she combats this problem.

"My work space has a north facing aspect & I work under the window, but I also use powerful daylight bulbs (4 in all) as well. To photograph my work I use a light box with a daylight bulb above, & one on each side. I prefer Fimo classic as I find it the most versatile. I never use acrylics for shading - always pastel powders as I find them more subtle & acrylics too heavy."

Someone who also uses artificial light, is **respected polymer clay colour expert Maggie Maggio** who uses full-spectrum OTT lights. She doesn't worry about the light her customers may display a piece in as she doesn't have to be as hung up about, and therefore can be more expressive with her colours than miniaturists .

She uses all the different clays for the structural characteristics that work the best for what she is doing at the time and adjusts the colours as she goes. "Sure it would be great if all brands came in great colors for mixing but that's not what we have available now".

Maggie believes that "[polymer] clay can imitate anything! The main thing is to be super observant and really look at how nature combines colors". Maggies Book Polymer Clay Colour Inspirations co-authored with Lindly Haunani really does what it says on the pack ... and then some.

I wanted to know how collectors approached the various problems caused by colour pigments, light and colour breakdown over time, all of which can affect colour, and perception of colour.

I asked Ahmed Al-thani, who is a prolific and respected miniatures collector, which lights he uses to display his collection, whether he is concerned about damage to his collection from light. And whether any of the pieces he has collected look disappointing in the light he is using, And if some look even better than when he bought them?

Ahmed's answer was refreshingly relaxed. And, in case the book has made the subject too serious, I am very happy to end the book on this note.

> "[Although] your research touches an important matter, to be honest I am not really worried about this so much.   The issue of discolouration of the miniatures I mean.
>
> I often like it when something has a faded or aged look.   Miniatures mimic real things in life and as such we ought to have things that belong in a flea market in miniature.
>
> I display my miniatures in their settings if that was available i.e. a doll's house room box and so on, and they would in that case be lit with the artists choice of lighting and I only switch them on when I am looking at them, which would be for a very short time every now and then. Otherwise I display them in glass cabinets and they would only be lit by the lights in the room which are chandeliers and spotlights.
>
> I will eventually display them publicly and then I would seek professional help and get the cold spotlights they use in the museum of Basel which have a very good and exhibit friendly lights.
>
> Kristin Baybars who has had her shop for more than 35 years has kept a window display since the late seventies exactly like it was.   So you can imagine as a result how much the sunlight has affected the toys.   I however find it extremely charming and value the antique looking toys a great deal.   It gives the items a quality which is impossible to attain with new toys and miniatures".

Index

ageing	40	flower petal	43-44	pineapple	44
almond	17,52	fluorescent	39,73	poinsettia	31
artichoke	67	forget me not	53,70	potato	45
asparagus	67	garlic	19,21	powder	24-25
aubergine	93	granite	91	prawn	35
autumn leaf	82	grapes	61	pumpkin	38,42-43,53
bacalao	94	grey	90	purple	17
baking	10	jamon	33	radicchio	12,21
banana	52	lavender	52,53	raspberry	26,53
basic colours	48	leeks	14	raw	67
beans	18-19,64-66	leftover	83,45	region	81
bleed	15,32	light	56-58	RGB	11,19,56-57
blend	13,75	lilac	53	rose	53
brassica	67	lines	12	sage	52,91
bug	73	liquid polymer	26	salmon	35
butter	45	lobster	34	salt	94
cactus	70	mackerel	15,75-77	scales	8
carrot	38,52	magenta	20-21	season	16,81
cheese	45	maize	52	setas	80
cherries	27-28	marble	91	shellfish	92
chestnut	12	marrow	39-41	Skinner shade	13,75
chorizo	32	meat mix	32,52	skins	12
Christmas red	31	metallic	73,95	spots	13
clams	92	metamerism	57	stalks	27
CMYK	11,19,56-57	mushroom	80	stem	63
cod	94	offset stacking	14	stone	91
colour bars	8	oil paint	26	strawberry	15,26,53
contrast	29	olive	53	stripes	12
cooked	67	onions	12	sweetcorn	52
coquinas	92	outline	30-31	tomatoes	29-30,43-44
crab	34	overcooked	67	translucent	60-61
cucurbit	42	paper bag	84-85	turnip	17
dragon fruit	20-21	pastels	25	varnish	93
Dulux	18	peacock	70	walnut	52
exaggeration	30-31	pearl-ex	73,95	wax	93
feather	70	pebbles	92	wood	86-87
figs	21	peppers	62-63		
fish	75-77	pigment	38		

Biography

Angie Scarr started playing with polymer clay in the mid 1980s when she was in her 20s but it was in 1989 after her daughter was born and she quit a job as a social work assistant that she took it up more seriously, initially making miniature foods as a complement to the work of her Mum, who was a dolls house enthusiast and miniature woodworker. Frustrated by the lumpen miniatures available at the time from all but a very few miniaturists, and inspired by the sight of a millefiori lemon slice, Angie accidentally made an orange cane by a different method than the one she'd seen. This design allowed her to re-enclose the cane into a full orange, and peel the skin back to make a realistic peeled fruit. And it was from this simple mistake and the addition of the Skinner Shade technique that she drew the inspiration which helped her to develop many ideas which, though innovative at the time are now part of the way miniatures are routinely made.

Her work is now often copied, and as Angie herself readily admits, regularly equalled and often improved upon. Angie however, now in her 60s, carries on innovating, solving three dimensional problems, finding short cuts and sharing inspirations and continues to have an influence on a new generation of miniature artists.

Thanks and Acknowledgements

Apart from the obvious help and inspiration and sometimes uncomfortable but kindly and invaluable criticism by my husband Frank, and the support and encouragement of my (now grown up) children, Dominic, Alan and Kira, thanks also go to:-

Daphne Robins for the B&Q trip to collect every Dulux colour chart ... and Dulux for obligingly and unwittingly providing the original inspiration for the 'underpinning' of this book.

Scott Tesler for his amazing CMYK colour charts I found on the internet. And to Michael Fitzmaurice for understanding why we couldn't afford to pay for his excellent design skills ... and giving us a few very useful pointers anyway.

To talented miniaturist friends far too numerous to mention but including Esperanza Rebollo, Mus and Yellow, Myoung Jang, Carmen Naran, Linda Cummings, and Ahmed Al Thani, who's generous support, inspiration and encouragement constantly humbles me. To Bil Wight for his clay gun adaption. And, because I keep forgetting but really do thank Marion Fancey for starting me off on the "Challenge Angie" series when she had my very early videos and when my first book was but an embryo!

Grateful thanks for generous help compiling the basic colour charts and for listening patiently to and answering my questions on colour, clay and pigments.

Tony Aquino, Van Aken - Kato clay (USA) and Paul Currie - Du-Kit clay (New Zealand)

Georges Desmare, and (Cernit demonstrator) Karen Walker - Cernit clay (Europe)

Iris Weiss Polyform products – Premo (USA)

To the Sennelier shop in Paris for their dedication to colour which annually 'boosts' me.

And, more recently, to Lindley Haunani and Maggie Maggio who's 'Polymer Clay Colour Inspirations' dropped on my doormat half way through the process of writing this book, and which, though it could have put me off trying to write another book about colour, in fact inspired me further!

Sources, resources & valuable reading for the colour 'geeks' among us!

Search "CMYK colour charts" for easy refernce numbers

Polymer Clay Colour Inspirations Haunani / Maggio **ISBN 978-0-8230-1501-6**

The Polymer Clay Artists Guide Segal **ISBN 978-1-77085-207-5**

Search "Free online test for colour acuity " to test your colour vision

Colour matching problems en.wikipedia.org/wiki/Metamerism_(color)

Mica shift ...The theory en.wikipedia.org/wiki/Birefringence

Premo Colour Charts
www.tooaquarius.com/tutorials/learn/colours/premo-ultramarine-blue-alizarin-crimson-cadmium-yellow/

Polymer Clay Suppliers

UK and Europe

theclayhub.co.uk Cernit

www.clay-and-paint.com Cernit

www.clayaround.com various clays

Fimo is widely available in craft shops in the UK & Europe

goedkoopsteklei.nl Holland

www.craftmill.co.uk Fimo and Premo

USA

www.polymerclayexpress.com stock all the major brands

Silver necklet by Clem with polymer clay inclusions by Angie (larger than actual size)

Basket by Isabel Franco Garcia with polymer clay vegetables by Angie

Coster Monger's hat shown at London Fashion Week 2008 by Stephen Jones Millinery with polymer clay fruit & vegetables by Angie

Patreon
Why I love my patrons

If you've never heard of Patreon before, imagine you could be a 'patron of the arts' in some small way helping your favourite artists to continue working, inventing and teaching in their specialist area. Artists no matter how well known in their field often have no regular guaranteed income and often give away their inspiration for free because until now there wasn't an easy method to gain an income from day to day teaching, support and skill sharing.

This subscription service is an easy way to connect artist teachers with their students and followers, and as a way for the 'patrons' to give the level of support they are comfortable with and receive in return (sometimes personalised) perks such as early access to new ideas, live patron only videos and little samples of work to help you visualise stages of work and qualities of colour. As well as advance knowledge of really new ideas before they ever get to publication. Some ideas of how I made things which never even reach the books which I call my 'daft ideas' for example how I made the awning for the dollhouse shop on the front just using parts from an old umbrella! For benefit patrons I'm also able to send out little found 'things' which might inspire you, or samples of my new tools before they go into full production.

Many thanks to my current 70+ patrons some of who have been with me for several years now. You've all given me courage to start with new things like this book. The Patreon thing has really helped me because it's like having 70 sets of shoulders to lean on. 70 therapists and 70 special friends to share my daft ideas with and see if they work. Or at least are interesting enough for you not to walk away! 70 people who understand that no matter how well known an artist is they still may struggle from time to time. That's worth so much!

www.patreon.com/angie_scarr

Making Miniature Food & Market Stalls
Angie's first book Published by Guild of Master Craftsman Publications. A bestselling introduction to making polymer clay miniature food. This is an updated edition.

Miniature Food Masterclass
Angie's second book with GMC. Also still a bestseller this one continues the journey of exploration into what polymer clay can replicate.

Other books by Sliding Scale

The Miniature Gardens Book
Have you ever fancied making more than just a flower garden in miniature? Angie gives you several garden styles and lots of new ideas.

The Dollhouse Flower Shop
This book concentrates on the innovative idea of stencilling flowers in polymer clay/liquid clay mix. Some equipment and materials are needed to get started.

3D Pen #1 Fairy Houses and Fantasy Gardens
A handy pattern book for anyone of any age who is looking for a project to make with their 3D pen. Excellent addition to a 3D pen gift.

Your Creative Business
Angie and SEO expert Kira share advice on all aspects of craft business from pricing and marketing through to multiple income streams to help you ensure a more secure future.

Your Creative Business Workbook
To go with the main book or as a stand alone. This workbook helps you decide on your business direction and includes ideas to improve your planning and profits.

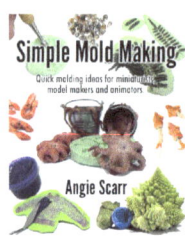

Simple Mold Making
Inspiration and unusual mould applications for polymer clay artists, miniaturists, animators, jewellery makers, cake decorators and many others.

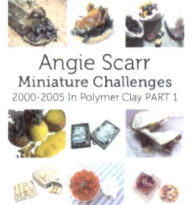

Angie Scarr Miniature Challenges Part 1
Revisiting all the old magazine articles in Dolls House and Miniature Scene and other dollhouse magazines most of which are otherwise out of print.

Angie Scarr Miniature Challenges Part 2
More old dolls house magazine articles revisited. Some with updated information.

Making it Small - Biography
Angie never lived an 'ordinary life'. When she and Frank met it became less ordinary still. A story of the love of crafts, miniatures, self building and life in a small pueblo in Spain.

The Frugalist
A look at revaluing your time, living better for less and gently preparing for unexpected crises. If life sometimes feel tough this book might just help.

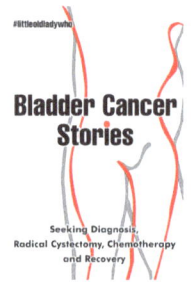

Bladder Cancer Stories
A personal, often humour filled journey through the downs and even ups of radical cystectomy and chemotherapy: back to health and a different view on life after bladder cancer.

www.angiescarr.com

For moulds, stencils, kits, books, miniatures and other craft materials
delivery worldwide

www.etsy.com/shop/AngieScarrCrafts
Our Etsy Digital store for plotter / cutter files. Flowers, leaves, boxes and a flowershop are among the designs.

www.patreon.com/angie_scarr
Support me and get sneak previews of my work and discounts in our shop.

www.facebook.com/angiescarr.miniatures
My facebook page where I let everyone know what is going on

www.instagram.com/angiescarr
Photos of work in progress

www.pinterest.co.uk/angiescarr
Links to my work all over the internet

ko-fi.com/angiescarr
Buy me a coffee

www.tiktok.com/@angiescarr
Video shorts

www.youtube.com/user/angiescarr
For tutorials, howtos and videos about crafts and miniatures